Daughter *of the* River Country

DIANNE O'BRIEN
WITH SUE WILLIAMS

**MANILLA
PRESS**

First published in Australia in 2021 by Echo Publishing,
an imprint of Bonnier Books UK
This edition published in the UK in 2021 by
MANILLA PRESS
An imprint of Bonnier Books UK
4th Floor, Victoria House, Bloomsbury Square, London WC1B 4DA
Owned by Bonnier Books
Sveavägen 56, Stockholm, Sweden

A CIP catalogue record for this book is
available from the British Library.

ISBN: 978–1–83877–579–7

Also available as an ebook and in audio

1 3 5 7 9 10 8 6 4 2

Page design and typesetting by Shaun Jury
Printed and bound in Great Britain by Clays Ltd, Elcograf S.p.A.

Manilla Press is an imprint of Bonnier Books UK
www.bonnierbooks.co.uk

*To my mum, Val Westman — if she'd lived long enough
to have seen this book, she would have been so proud*

Contents

Foreword

Growing up, it seemed like we had a good life. I had a wonderful mother who loved me, a dad who took me fishing, an older half-brother who looked out for me, and lots of mates. Mum was the centre of my world and taught me everything I needed to know, and then some. Everyone loved her and, in turn, she helped me understand how important it was to care for others. As a family, we weren't rich, but we weren't dirt poor, either. Mum worked hard all her life on farms and Dad earnt a decent living as a truckie and a bootmaker.

Later on, I discovered nearly everything had been a lie, and my world crumbled. My mother wasn't my mother. My father wasn't my father. My half-brother was absolutely no relation to me. I wasn't Irish-Australian like my parents. My name wasn't even Dianne Westman. I was actually Aboriginal and part of the Stolen

Generation. I was a daughter of the river country and, as everyone who knows just a small part of my story says, it's a miracle I'm still alive today.

PART ONE
LOST

Chapter One
Jealousy's Poison

I don't know exactly when my father started hating me.

Early on, I like to think he didn't. I have so many old photographs of us fishing together, playing together, laughing together. There I am, beaming at the camera, and there he is, looking down fondly at me, his only child. In some photos, he has his arm around me. In others, he has my hand in his.

But then, at some point, things changed. I've spent a long time trying to figure out why. What did I do wrong? What could a child possibly do to turn her father into an enemy? I asked myself this every time he flogged me with the buckle end of his belt. And I asked myself again when Mum warned me never to be alone with him.

I realised later that it was my mother who'd taken all those photos. Dad had been on his best behaviour while she was watching.

But as I grew older, those happy childhood days of fun and love and innocence gradually darkened into nights of fear and despair. My father almost destroyed my life. Almost.

My family was pretty average, no different than anyone else's. I was born 3 July 1946 at the Wagga Wagga Base Hospital, in what is the largest inland city in NSW, halfway between Sydney and Melbourne, about 450 kilometres from each. Back then, it was the centre of the war effort, with an air force base, an army camp, and thousands of troops stationed there for training. Before I came along Mum did her bit as a member of the Women's Auxiliary Australian Air Force (WAAAF). That was typical of her, always helping others.

Her name was Val Westman, and she was softly spoken and pretty with a pale complexion, fine features and dark-brown hair that shone gold in the sun. She'd worked from a young age on wheat farms in the country, doing back-breaking tasks in the fields, cooking for the other farmhands, and sewing wheat bags. She'd been married before she met my dad and had a son, my half-brother Ronnie, who was six years older than me. Apparently, Mum's first husband was mean and used to beat her up. One of my uncles told me that he'd once seen him dragging her along the floor by her hair. I was horrified at the thought of anyone doing such terrible things to my beautiful mother, but she never mentioned it. I think she wanted to do everything she could to shield me from the ugly side of life.

When I was little, we lived on a wheat farm in Parkes, about 260 kilometres north of Wagga Wagga in central west NSW. Parkes had its own RAAF station during the war, in a region that had mines dating back to the old gold rush days, and was surrounded by wool and wheat farms. The WAAAF closed down the year after I was born and Mum worked on the farm full-time, alongside my dad, George Westman. When he wasn't doing farm work, he was a truck driver, transporting diesel and other fuels around the country and earning good money.

Dad was a handsome man and was proud of his dark good looks. He had a natural charisma and I adored him, nearly as much as I adored my mother. He'd take me to the truck park to look at the big rigs and sometimes even let me ride in the cab with him. On his days off, when Mum was busy with Ronnie, he'd take me fishing or crabbing by torchlight. He didn't like seeing Mum and Ronnie together and I think he was jealous, although it seemed strange that an adult could be jealous of a kid. He often picked on Ronnie and complained whenever Mum bought him anything, saying she was spoiling him. But maybe Mum simply wanted to make up for Ronnie having such a bad dad.

When I was three years old, because of Dad's trucking job, we moved to Granville in Sydney, a working-class suburb out west. It was a knockabout kind of place and in those days still very much on the city's outskirts. It was originally called Parramatta Junction because it was the final stop on the first railway line in NSW from Sydney to Parramatta. Our little weatherboard house on Redfern Street had a big verandah closed in by glass shutters, an outside dunny and a back garden where we grew vegetables and kept chooks. The house was at the back of the Crest Theatre, surrounded by paddocks and close to where the travelling circus set up every year.

Mum and Dad both had Irish ancestry and had family in the area, so I had lots of uncles and aunts and cousins. Mum's brothers, the Callaghans, were illegal bookmakers and she often worked with them, delivering little yellow envelopes full of money all around Sydney, sometimes getting me to help. It seemed, through them, we were 'connected'. My godfather was none other than underworld gambling kingpin Lenny McPherson, who later became a notorious standover man said to have committed, and commissioned, more murders than any other organised crime figure in Sydney. We had a photo of him attending my christening. Although he was a godfather of crime, he wasn't much of one to me. I don't remember ever seeing him again. My godmother was an old friend of Mum's, Joy, from Parkes, but I never met her, either.

*

Mum was sociable and had loads of friends. She loved it when people came over to play cards and for sing-songs around the piano with one of my uncles on his squeezebox and another on a mouth organ. Sometimes I'd join them on the spoons. And if I didn't, invariably at some point she'd halt everything.

'Dianne, darling!' she'd call out. 'Come over here and give us a song! You've got a lovely voice. Sing us one of our favourites from the old country. You can pick which one.'

I'd squirm in my seat, blushing and embarrassed, and shake my head. There was no escape. I'd take a deep breath and sing and gradually everyone else would join in. In truth, I loved music and harboured a secret longing one day to be a professional singer.

Dad didn't join in much and I remember thinking he was resentful somehow of Mum's popularity and how close I was to her. He didn't have many friends and didn't see much of his family. I was curious to meet them, especially as he had a niece, the daughter of his sister, also called Dianne Westman. But I don't think his family particularly liked him. We'd occasionally meet an aunt or uncle, he'd have a row with them and then we'd never see them again. Dad would go to the local pub, the Royal, with Mum on occasions, and I suppose they both drank, although they never did that at home in front of me.

With Dad away on the road a lot of the time, Mum was the centre of my world. She had a little black Scottish Terrier, Danny, who was devoted to her too and followed her everywhere, as well as a pet parrot, Clarrie, which she taught to talk, call for her, swear and sing Irish songs. Mum had such a big heart; she also helped out a number of families in the area, taking care of their kids when they couldn't. She was so good at it, the Child Welfare Department – the government organisation in charge of kids – asked her to look after one of theirs.

But she always had time for me and Ronnie. She made all our clothes, and she even created my favourite rag doll Molly, using her own hair, that I carried around everywhere from the age of two. She taught us about God and the difference between right and wrong, told us we should always stand up for ourselves and our rights, and warned me never ever to swear. If I did, she said,

I'd end up in Parramatta Girls Home for wayward girls. It was a threat delivered in such a menacing voice, I imagined it must be the worst place on earth.

Later I discovered it truly was.

But back then, life was a dream. Mum cooked for us every day and taught me how to cook, too, and how to clean. She was so house-proud and was always sweeping and scrubbing and polishing and washing, and impressed upon me, even at that young age, how important it was to keep things neat and tidy. 'You never know who's going to come visiting,' she'd say.

I'd assumed she meant family and friends until the first time an inspector from child welfare called round. This woman wandered about our house, trailing her finger along every surface. I could sense how tense Mum was until the woman finally nodded to her, turned and left. After that, I never complained when Mum asked me to help with the housework. I didn't understand, but I knew it must be for a good cause.

*

Every summer, we'd go camping in Budgewoi on the Central Coast, about 110 kilometres north of Sydney. While Mum, Dad and Ronnie spent their time sitting on the beach and occasionally going for a paddle in the ocean, I discovered I loved swimming.

'You're a real water baby,' Mum would say to me as I begged to be allowed to go swimming every morning. 'Don't you get sick of it?'

'No, Mum,' I said. 'I love it. It just feels great being in the water.'

Dad would laugh. 'I remember the first time I put you in the lake. You went straight down and I thought that was you – gone! I was just coming to rescue you when you bobbed up again. You learnt how to swim underwater before you learnt to swim on top of it.'

It was a story I'd heard many times before, but I never tired of it. It was true. Somehow, when the water closed over my head, I felt peaceful. When I ran out of air, I just kicked my way back up to the surface. Mum had been terrified, and berated Dad for letting me go in alone. But it was the start of my lifelong love for the water. I was never so keen on the beach, though, and would much prefer to swim in the Budgewoi Lake or Lake Munmorah, to the north. Depending on the tides and rain, and the height of the rivers and streams that drained into the lagoons, they were a lot less salty. I much preferred freshwater. I was a real river girl.

At the age of six, I started at the local Catholic primary school. It was hard at first: I didn't like being separated from Mum and the nuns picked on me. I thought I was well-behaved but I kept getting the cane. Sometimes I felt like the nuns were tormenting me just for the fun of it. One time, Mum hadn't paid the schoolbook fee that was due and the nuns caned me long and hard on my hands. Mum marched straight down to the school and complained. Another time, I was caned on my hands and on the backs of my legs because my school fees hadn't been paid. It turned out Mum hadn't even received the letter saying that they were due, and so she went down there again in my defence. They had an almighty row that day and Mum came home in tears. I was devastated and put my arms around her. She never said exactly what happened, but I overheard my aunt and uncle whispering that the nuns didn't like us because we were Irish and poor. I was shocked to think that adults would behave that way. It didn't seem right.

When I tried to protest, Mum hushed me. 'Oh Dianne, you'll learn the hard way.' It was something she was to repeat whenever anything went wrong in my life. Looking back, she was right. Somehow, she knew.

One day, there was a loud knocking on the front door and Danny started barking. Mum didn't answer it, so I dragged a chair to the door and stood on it so I could reach the top lock. As soon as the lock clicked open, a man burst in, knocking me off the chair. Mum heard the commotion and came running out but then stopped dead in her tracks at the sight of our visitor. She looked frozen in fear. The man seized our best vase off a shelf and, to my absolute horror, smashed it over Mum's head. She fell to the floor and my blood turned to ice.

I was crying and Danny was barking madly and racing in circles around Mum. But the man kicked him to one side, shouted something and then ran off. I went straight over and tried to help Mum sit up. The whole episode had only lasted a few seconds, but it had been terrifying. Mum told me to say nothing about it and we never spoke of it again. I learnt years later that our visitor was Mum's first husband.

I never answered the front door again without checking who was there.

That incident was one of the reasons Mum agreed I could have my own dog. We'd been standing out the front of our house when we saw one of the men from the visiting circus carrying a hessian bag over his shoulder. The bag was moving and wriggling and Mum called out to him to ask what he had. He put the bag down and beckoned us over. Inside the bag was a litter of puppies that the man said were half-dingo and half-wolf.

'She can have one if she wants,' he said, jerking his head towards me.

'Oh Mum, please can I have one?' I begged. '*Please?*'

At that point, Dad came out of the house to see what all the fuss was about. The men had a word together and Dad nodded.

'Okay, but only if she promises to look after it,' he said.

I hugged Mum with delight. 'This is the best day of my life!'

From that moment on, just like Mum with Danny, I had a dog, Lassie, who followed me everywhere. I was overjoyed. She instantly won over Danny, and even Clarrie the parrot soon started mimicking her bark in between her calls and songs. I don't think Dad was all that pleased about the constant noise in the house.

A few weeks later, not far off my seventh birthday, I came home from school and found Mum crying. She was too upset to tell me what was wrong but the house was strangely silent. I glanced towards the back verandah and saw a small black body lying there. It was Danny. I raced over and tried to rouse him, but he didn't stir. Mum was so distressed, Dad had to call the doctor to see her, and she stayed in bed for weeks.

It took her a long time to recover. She'd spend hours sitting quietly in the house, or just lying in bed. I was so worried about her and secretly terrified we might lose her, too. One night, I had a terrible dream about a crocodile that turned into a shark and started chasing me. Crying, I tried to sneak into bed beside Mum. Dad woke up, pulled back the covers and lifted me in between them both. For a moment, I was aware of their warm bodies either side of mine, and pleased that he'd been happy to let me into their bed. Then I felt him take my hand and put it between his legs. I didn't know what was happening but it felt wrong. I was too petrified to move and started to cry again. As soon as he let my hand go, I leapt out of that bed as if it were on fire and scampered back to my room.

From that moment on, nothing was ever the same again.

Chapter Two
Feeling Different

I never told anyone what happened that night in Mum and Dad's bed; I didn't know how to. I was too young to really understand but I knew that it had felt wrong, horribly wrong. I didn't want to upset my mum further by saying something, and I was suddenly scared of my dad. It made me feel different to the other kids in my street. Despite having Lassie constantly by my side, following me to school, waiting at the bus stop for me to get home again and sharing every ice cream I ever had, I started to feel lonely.

There was no respite. Some nights I had nightmares about being chased by that shark and would wake up in a cold sweat just as it caught up with me. I was frightened but I didn't dare creep into Mum and Dad's bed again. I also began sleepwalking. That didn't really bother me, but I know it worried Mum.

Dad still took me out occasionally in his truck, but now I was wary. We'd go to my favourite place in the world – the Granville pool – but I'd be careful to swim on my own in the deep end where he rarely ventured. He loved wrestling and boxing, but Mum hated that sort of thing, so he'd take me instead to watch bouts in Newtown. Whenever we went, I'd make sure we were with other people. I'd always loved it when he took me out for a drive and drove fast, but now I'd sit in the back to urge him on. I stopped going to his truck yard after the time all the men were drinking and I noticed one of them playing with himself. Again, I didn't understand what he was doing, but I knew I didn't like it. Dad just laughed at my confusion.

Mum lost some of her spirit after Danny's death, and she often looked sad and sick. I'd try everything I could to make her smile. I'd dress up and play the fool; I'd tie my wiry shock of black hair back and smooth it down away from my face, just like she always said I should; I'd put on the white top that was her favourite instead of the multi-coloured one in Spanish colours – red, yellow and black – that I loved more. Sometimes my friends would come over and we'd clown around until we got Mum to smile. It felt like the sun coming out after a very dark storm. But she was spending more time in bed and the doctor said her heart was wearing out from a lifetime of hard physical work. So I couldn't spend too much time with her in case it made her too tired.

Six years older than me and a teenager now, my half-brother Ronnie didn't really want to be bothered by his kid sister. I asked Mum once if she could give me some more siblings. I'd always dreamt about being part of a big family and having five sisters –

that would have been perfect. Some kids in the neighbourhood, especially those with similar Irish blood, had lots of brothers and sisters and I envied them. But Mum just shook her head. She said she'd had a problem with a pregnancy and was sorry, but she couldn't have any more children. She showed me a big scar on her belly and said that was the result of having a baby in her tubes. I'd have to be content with her and Dad and Ronnie.

'I'm sorry,' she said, putting her arm around me. 'I know it's lonely and that you always wanted sisters. But it does make you even more special to us.'

I must have pulled a face because she looked despondent and I immediately felt mean. 'That's all right, Mum,' I replied, trying to put on a cheerier face. 'It doesn't matter.'

She was silent for a moment. 'But Dianne, I do have something for you, and for you alone.'

I was puzzled. 'What?'

'No, not now. But soon I'm going to take you on a trip back to Parkes, where we used to live. Then I'm going to sit you down and tell you something, a secret.'

'What kind of secret?' I whined.

'A very special secret,' she said, smiling. 'But we have to go to Parkes for me to tell you. Until then ...' she put her finger to her lips, 'you have to wait.'

Despite feeling unwell, Mum took in ironing for ten shillings a basket and continued looking after other kids. I suddenly realised that she was saving up for our big trip to the country! I followed her example and started doing babysitting around the neighbourhood on the weekends. I loved children and I loved helping out their parents. Sometimes I pretended they were my own little brothers and sisters to make up for the hole in my heart. I saved my money too. But I wondered what on earth Mum wanted to tell me when we got to Parkes.

*

Dad was driving trucks less now and one of Mum's brothers, Uncle Walter, parked his caravan in our backyard and started living there. He was a bootmaker and taught Dad how to make them too to earn some extra money. Dad proved good at it and everyone started calling me 'the bootmaker's daughter'. But he didn't share much of his earnings with Mum. When she asked him for more, he'd say no, because she might give it to Ronnie.

Our cousins lived in Newtown in the Inner West, six kids squashed into one bedroom, and they always looked threadbare and poor. Their dad, my Uncle Ken, who was actually Mum's nephew, was often sick and spent a lot of time in hospital, so he couldn't work much. Mum would make me give them my old clothes – which I resented as she'd made them especially for me – and she'd tell Dad to take our cousins vegetables from our big plot in the back garden. He'd dutifully drive over to Newtown with a basket full of fresh produce. It was only later I found out that instead of doing the right thing, he was actually selling the vegetables to our family!

Mum would save a little bit out of the cash Dad gave her by shopping in Auburn, a few kilometres away where the groceries were cheaper and she could use food stamps. She'd tell Dad that the food cost four pounds when really it had just cost two, or a dress cost three pounds when it really only cost a pound fifty, so she could put away the leftovers. I knew she was planning for our big trip.

It didn't seem fair that she had to scrimp and save all the time when she was sick and had always worked so hard. The hurt inside me started building up. Occasionally, it would erupt in bursts of temper. I never quite understood what made me snap. Mum had always told me how important it was to stand up for myself, but sometimes it was impossible. I couldn't stand up for myself against my dad. And I couldn't defy the nuns at school who seemed to have pinned a target on my back.

One time, I was in the playground and had my head down, pretending to charge at a mate like a bull. He stepped aside at the last minute and I accidentally head-butted the nun behind him, right in her stomach. For that, I got another thrashing with the cane. It was so unfair. I ran back to the playground and in a fit of anger set the rubbish inside the school bin on fire and tipped it over. I didn't really think of what might happen, but the fire spread to the leaves lying on the grass and soon half the playground lawn was ablaze. I got the cane for that, too, but this time I didn't care. At least I'd earnt it!

Soon after, I left the nuns at that Catholic school and started going to a different primary school nearby. Mum was worried and told me I should behave myself, otherwise I'd end up – as per the usual threat – in Parramatta Girls Home.

*

In 1956, television came to Granville, and all us kids would pile into a neighbour's house down the road who had the area's first TV set. I'd always loved going to the pictures and I quickly found I loved TV too. It was a great escape. A favourite show of ours was *The Mickey Mouse Club*. One day we were all watching when one of the Mouseketeers came on, a darker-skinned Italian American girl called Annette Funicello.

'That's you!' one of my friends shouted. 'Look!'

Everyone started shrieking with laughter. I peered at the screen in confusion. What did she mean? I wasn't Italian; I was Irish. 'Don't be stupid,' I said, sharply. 'She doesn't look *anything* like me.'

'Yes she does!' yelled a couple of my friends in unison. 'She's your spitting image. Bloody hell. Look at her!'

I did, but I couldn't see any resemblance at all. She had dark skin, and I was much paler and, I felt, no different from any of my friends. 'You don't know what you're talking about,' I said, annoyed. 'Now shut up and watch the show.'

I spent the rest of the day bewildered, mulling it over. Sadly, Funicello was one of the most popular Mouseketeers and appeared regularly. Every time she came on, we went through the same rigmarole: everyone saying that she was my double, and me insisting she wasn't.

From that point on, whenever there was a show with someone with darker skin, the chorus would chime that it was me again. I was so hurt. I didn't think I looked any different to anyone else, so why were they picking on me? Mum and Dad didn't look any different to all of the other parents in the street, so what on earth were they going on about?

When I came home one Saturday after babysitting, Mum was waiting for me. 'Close your eyes,' she said. 'We have a surprise for you!' I closed my eyes and she guided me into the lounge room. Then she said I could look. There was a box covered by a cloth, which she whisked away triumphantly. It was a TV! We had our own TV set! We were the fourth family in Granville to get one. Now I could watch at home with the pick of my closest friends who wouldn't tease me about the colour of my skin.

I wasn't so lucky. In 1957, the black American actress and singer Diahann Carroll started appearing on the US TV variety program, *The Ed Sullivan Show*.

'Whoa!' said one of my friends the first time we saw her. 'Look at her! Anyone recognise her?'

I looked at her blankly, until my friend started roaring with laughter and everyone else soon joined in. 'No?' I said. 'What do you mean?'

'Look in the mirror!' my friend yelled.

'Yeah,' another one said. 'It's her all right!'

My half-brother Ronnie came in to see what all the clamour was about and I hoped he might defend me. No way. 'Yep,' he said. 'She was even named Dianne after her 'cos we thought they looked so alike.'

I stared at him. 'That's impossible,' I said. 'We've never even seen her or heard of her before now.' He just smiled and left the room.

I didn't know many black people, apart from one boy in the

neighbourhood called Greg Peckham who was Aboriginal and mad on sport and was always wandering around with a football under his arm. He was nice and I nicknamed him my 'black tracker' as he often turned up on the street when I was there. But while I had nothing against him or other Aboriginal people, I didn't want to be thought of as one. I wanted to be like everyone else. Most people didn't seem to like people with darker skin. There was a lot of discrimination in those days and the White Australia Policy kept overseas people of colour out. It'd be ten years before Aborigines were included in the census, sixteen years before the government got rid of the White Australia Policy and another two years before there were laws against racism.

It all made me feel even more isolated from the other kids. I kept a diary, religiously, from around the age of eight. Sometimes I'd sit in our backyard with Lassie and tell her how lonely and how 'different' I was and how I suddenly felt that I no longer belonged. She'd listen to me patiently and I knew that at least she'd love me no matter what I looked like.

My best friend was a boy called Brian who had a big family where there was always a lot going on. I met him through his sister Shirley who was also a close friend, and we instantly clicked. I loved listening to his stories about his brothers and sisters and the things they got up to. He would come and help me clean the house for half my pocket money. At weekends, we'd collect beer bottles together and cash them in for money to go to the pictures. On my tenth birthday in 1956, we cut our wrists and put them together so the blood would mingle, making us forever blood brother and sister.

But it turned out I couldn't rely on my blood brother. One day, we had a silly argument about carrying schoolbooks home. He yelled at me and called me a 'black bitch'. I was outraged and upset and just saw red. I hated him. Without knowing what I was doing, I picked up half a house brick lying in the gutter and thumped him in the head. He ran off crying, blood dripping from the wound. Later that day, his mum came round to see my mum. Mum simply couldn't believe I'd done anything like that to my closest friend. Neither could I.

But worse was to come. Much, much worse.

Chapter Three
Fighting Back

Brian was remorseful and I knew he regretted being so nasty to me, and not only because his head hurt for days afterwards. I started giving him a wide berth and I think he missed my company. He did seem genuinely sorry and apologised every time he saw me. In truth, I missed him too. His sister Shirley tried to smooth over our rift, but I felt so let down by someone I'd thought of as my brother, my one true friend, that I found it hard to forgive him.

You needed allies, though, in our neighbourhood. It was a rough and tough sort of place, the kind of cheap area of Sydney where hard-up people from the country would come to work in the factories and move into whatever Housing Commission houses were on offer. As a result, there'd often be strangers around who were down on their luck. Mum warned me always to be careful.

Turned out she was the first to fall victim and it was all my fault. I was still only ten and one night about midnight, I went sleepwalking again. Even though Mum was in the habit of locking the front door to stop me getting out, apparently I undid the lock – while still asleep – and went wandering down the road in my nightdress. Mum must have heard the bolt go and she came running out after me in her dressing gown, with Lassie in hot pursuit.

Just as she caught up to me, a car driving up the road stopped and two men got out, grabbed her and tried to bundle her into their car. Her terrified screaming and Lassie's manic barking woke me up and I started shouting too. Suddenly Dad was on the scene, pushing the men aside and pulling Mum back. The men leapt into their car and raced away. Dad took us back to the house, promising he'd put extra bolts high up on the door to stop me sleepwalking out into the neighbourhood again.

It was even tricky during the daytime for us kids. A few weeks later, I was coming home from school when two older boys jumped me from behind. I hadn't even seen them approach, but they got me down on the ground and one kneeled on my shoulders while the other one put his hands up my skirt and tried to pull down my knickers.

I screamed and struggled and fought back and must have made such a row that I could then hear someone shouting and heavy footsteps coming towards us. After a split-second, I recognised the voice: it was Brian! He wrenched one of the boys away and then hit the other one full in the face. That boy swore and let me go and ran off while Brian kicked the other one for luck. He then pulled me up and dusted me off. I fell, sobbing, into his arms. I couldn't keep giving him the cold shoulder after that.

'Are you all right, Di?' he asked, when I'd caught my breath. 'They didn't ...?'

'No,' I reassured him. 'They'd only just started when you came. Thanks so much!'

'Aw, that's nothing,' he said. 'Glad I could help. I didn't recognise them, did you?'

'No, but I didn't really get a good look. I was just trying so hard to get them off me.'

'Di, I just wanted to say sorry again for what I said before.'

'That's fine. Forget it.'

He looked relieved. 'Okay. Now I'm going to sort you out for the future.'

True to his word, the next day two of the toughest boys in the neighbourhood came knocking at my door. They were the Harrisons, from a family of boxers and fearsome streetfighters.

'Brian says you could do with a hand, learning to fight,' one of them said. 'So we're here to teach you.'

*

Mum wasn't happy I was learning how to fight. Always an elegant lady herself, I think she hoped I'd grow up to be the same.

I was developing early and by the age of eleven I looked more like I was fourteen. I knew boys were noticing me. I liked to look pretty and dress nicely but at the same time I kept up my lessons with Kenny and Billy Harrison. I learnt to punch and kick and wrestle someone to the ground, and how to get away when someone was doing the same to me. The Harrisons were impressed at my progress and I think took pride in their pupil.

Sydney's western suburbs in those days were ruled by an assortment of gangs who each had their own area, and woe betide you if you crossed into someone else's patch. I started to earn a reputation as one of the best girl fighters around. Mind you, if you turned up at a neighbourhood brawl with one of the Harrisons in tow, most of the work was done for you. They'd take one look at me, then look at Kenny or Billy, and vanish in a cloud of dust.

If any gang from another suburb came to Granville and started bullying kids, taking their pocket money or bashing them, we three would go and sort them out. Sometimes girls from other areas would come and take a look at me to see if they'd be able to beat me. I quickly found that acting tough and unafraid would intimidate them. But when the chips were down and I did have to fight, I'd throw everything I had at it.

I surprised myself with how well I fought. It was like I had a deep seam of anger somewhere inside that just exploded. Friends said my eyes would go dark, almost black, and then I'd let rip. Maybe it was anger at Dad, or anger that my beloved mum was having such a hard life, or anger that I felt so different to everyone else. Whatever it was, I'd lose track of what I was doing and sometimes wouldn't even remember what had happened afterwards. But I soon realised these fights were good for me because they allowed me to channel all my anger and take it out on other people. I was still innocent and trusting, but now I knew I could defend myself, or at least give it a hell of a good shot.

I still loved music and dancing and Mum tried to steer me towards those less dangerous activities. She bought me a little pink-and-black record player and I spent hours alone in my bedroom listening to a new singer who'd just appeared by the name of Elvis Presley. I adored him. 'Heartbreak Hotel', 'Blue Suede Shoes', 'I Love You Because', 'Tutti Frutti', 'One-Sided Love Affair' ... Elvis had risen from poverty to become a star and was known to be generous and kind, and I felt he was singing just to me. I saved everything I could – posters, newspaper articles, photos – in my Elvis collection.

Sometimes I'd meet up with friends at the Crest Theatre and we'd watch an Elvis movie and dance in the aisle until the usher made us go back to our seats. Other times we'd gather at the swimming pool or a milk bar and then we'd all go to someone's house to practise our rock 'n' roll dancing. Mum was happy to see me do that, although often she assumed we were going to do our school homework together rather than spending the whole evening listening to music and dancing. She liked to Charleston and would have preferred me to have taken up ballet, but anything was better than fighting.

Occasionally, when we had the money, we'd go to Blacktown to see the singers we'd been watching on the TV pop show *Bandstand*, people like Johnny Devlin, known as New Zealand's answer to Elvis, or the Australians Col Joye and Dig Richards, the lead singer with the R'Jays. Sometimes they'd perform in Parramatta, so we'd follow them there, too. On Saturday nights, there'd be a dancing competition at the Auburn Community Hall and we'd all compete. My partner was an overweight boy who could dance and swing you around and throw you over his shoulders and under his legs better than anyone.

One day, Mum called me over. 'Hey, I've got a surprise for you,' she said. 'I think it's about time you learnt to play something other than the spoons. I've been talking to our new neighbour. He's got a guitar and is pretty handy with it. I thought I might pay for a few lessons.'

'Wow, Mum, that'd be great!'

'Well, go round there this afternoon and ask him how much he'll charge. I don't think it'll be too much. I'll pay from some of the money I've saved up for our trip to Parkes.'

I was thrilled and did a little Elvis dance with an imaginary air guitar to make Mum laugh. Then I hugged her.

'Thanks, Mum,' I said.

That afternoon, I knocked on the neighbour's door and a handsome black man opened it. He shook my hand warmly. 'Ah, you're Val's daughter, Dianne,' he said. 'My name's Jimmy Little. I've been expecting you. Come in.'

As we went into his lounge room he picked up a guitar and handed me another one.

'Have you ever played before?' he asked.

'No,' I said, shyly. 'But I've listened to them heaps.'

He laughed. 'Then that should stand you in good stead.'

'But I have to ask you how much you'll charge,' I said,

remembering suddenly what Mum had said. 'It might be too much …'

'Listen, darling,' he said, putting his hand on my shoulder. 'When you can play like me, that's when you can pay. Until then, I'll teach you for free.'

Jimmy loved country music and said his big influences were Nat King Cole, Johnny Mathis and Jim Reeves, but he wrote and performed all his own songs. Secretly, I knew I'd never be as good as him on guitar, and I think he knew it too, and that I'd never end up paying him. He had a soft spot for kids from families who were obviously battlers, but he seemed to take a particular shine to me.

He told me he was Aboriginal, a Yorta Yorta man from a place he called the Cummeragunja Aboriginal Reserve on the Murray River in New South Wales, near Echuca. He was obviously proud of where he came from and his heritage. His people's totem was a long-necked turtle and he said they were responsible for looking after the water the turtles lived in. He asked me if I liked the water and I said I loved it; the pool was my favourite place in the world.

It was the first time I'd got to know an Aboriginal person and I found him a lovely man, very warm and very kind. He had a wife and a little daughter, Frances Clarrie, and I'd often see them down in the local park together. Jimmy worked in a towelling factory by day but had also signed a record deal and had a single out called 'Francis Clarrie', and then another one, 'Give the Coloured Boy a Chance', which he told me his dad had written and was the first song ever released in Australia about Aborigines. To my excitement, he became a bit of a regular on *Bandstand*, and another single, a recording of 'Danny Boy', stormed up the charts.

I quickly became Jimmy Little's biggest fan. But it puzzled me why other people weren't as enthusiastic and proud of his success. My Uncle Dick, for instance, didn't seem to like anyone with dark skin. A cousin had a girlfriend who was Indian and Uncle Dick wouldn't let her in his house. He used to make us kids show just our hand through the front door before he'd allow us in. Sometimes he'd even hesitate over my hand as it was darker than my cousins'. Then at night, down the pub, Uncle Dick would pick fights with Aboriginal men and kick them into the gutter. I just didn't understand it.

Spending time with Jimmy and my mates, playing music, listening to music and dancing to music, didn't mean I stayed out of trouble, though. One Saturday evening when I came home, Mum was standing at the front door with her arms crossed and a face like thunder.

'Hi Mum!' I said, instantly feeling nervous. She wasn't angry with me very often. I'd even tied my hair back with a piece of gauze scarf, the way she always asked me to, as she didn't like it when I wore my hair down all around my face. 'What's up?'

'Where have you been till this time, Dianne?' she asked, stiffly.

'I was at Shirley's, doing my maths homework.'

She scowled and my heart lurched. 'Try again. And think carefully this time before you say anything.'

I hesitated. I'd actually been at ABC TV's Gore Hill studios for *Six O'Clock Rock*, the rock 'n' roll show hosted by Johnny

O'Keefe, where I'd danced the evening away in the audience with my mates. I weighed up quickly whether Mum could have found out and decided there was no way.

'We had a *lot* of homework and ...'

She butted in. 'Go to your room. We don't tell lies in this house.'

'But Mum ...' I started.

'Don't "but Mum" me. I know exactly where you were. You were at *Six O'Clock Rock*. You lied to me. I'm so disappointed in you, Dianne. I don't want you ever to lie to me again.'

I slunk past her and went to my bedroom, tears stinging my eyes. I felt terrible having lied to the most important person in my world, and even worse that I'd been caught out.

I never could work out how Mum knew. It wasn't until years later when I was idly watching an old black-and-white recording of Johnny O'Keefe singing in the show in 1959 on YouTube that I suddenly caught sight of myself, with that gauze scarf in my hair, rock 'n' rolling right in front of the TV camera. Mum had obviously been watching and had seen me as clear as day.

That was the first and last time I ever told her a lie. I tortured myself horribly about it.

Little did I know she'd been lying to me my whole life.

Chapter Four
Doesn't Dianne Know?

The more I went out with my mates – swimming, dancing and having a good time – the more Dad seemed to get angry. I'd started high school and was doing well at my lessons and winning my races at swimming carnivals, but he started picking on me for everything and anything. I'd complain to Mum but she'd just tell me to try to avoid him whenever he was in a bad temper.

But even when he was in a good mood, it wasn't easy. As I walked past him at home, he started pinching me on the bottom, and he'd talk about my body shape and how I was so quickly becoming a woman. I hated it. As a typical thirteen-year-old, I was self-conscious, and having someone draw attention to my body in such an obviously sleazy way made me feel worse. He seemed to go out of his way to embarrass me.

'Look at those headlights!' he'd say in a loud voice, pointing to my breasts. 'That's a fine set you're getting there, m'girl.' And then he'd tweak my nipples like a bicycle horn.

Other times, he'd talk dirty to me, using words I didn't understand. I just knew it made me feel uncomfortable inside. But it got worse. One Saturday morning, I was playing football with some of my mates in the park. Dad was there on the sidelines and wanted me for something and called out, but I was in the middle of the game and didn't hear him. He came up behind me and the first I knew of it was when I felt a blow across the back of my head.

I turned round, my fists up ready to defend myself, and then saw it was my dad. I dropped them in confusion. 'Dad!' I said. 'What ...?'

'You slut!' he shouted. 'I'll teach you to ignore me! You're a slut, you hear me?' And then he dragged me home.

When Mum came back from the shops, she found me crying in my room. I told her what Dad had done. 'What's a slut? Why did he call me that?'

'Oh Dianne. I don't know what's the matter with him.'

'But what's a slut?' I persisted.

She sighed. 'A slut ... a slut is what they call a woman who goes with men.'

'Goes *where* with men?' I asked, confused.

'No, I mean a woman who has sex with lots of men. Who doesn't have any morals. A woman who's ... easy.'

I still didn't really understand but nodded as if I did. It obviously wasn't a nice thing. 'Why would he say that to me?'

'I don't know, Dianne,' she said, tiredly. 'He just loves you. But be careful when you're with him, okay?'

That afternoon, a friend of mine, Vicki, called round. Her dad was bashing her, so she'd decided to run away from home. I made a snap decision and said I'd come too. I put a few things in a plastic bag and headed out with her, to catch a train into the city. From there, we caught another train to North Sydney and explored the big shopping centre and the surrounding neighbourhood for a few hours.

At first, it was great fun. We slept the night in a park, and it was new and exciting and an adventure. But then the next day seemed to drag. We wandered around North Sydney some more and then entered the grounds of a school and decided to sleep there for our second night. Just as it was getting dark, a man walked up to us, started chatting and then asked if we'd like to go back to his flat. I said no, but Vicki said yes, and they began kissing.

I felt uneasy but Vicki said it was fine. She was older than me, sixteen, and she'd done 'stuff' with men before, she said, and I just needed to grow up. I wondered if this was what 'slut' meant. I got scared and started thinking about Mum and how worried she'd be. I'd run away to get back at Dad, but now I panicked I'd be hurting Mum more. I rang her from a telephone booth and she begged me to come straight home. So I left Vicki with the man and their kissing and caught the next train home to Granville. I thought that however hard Dad beat me, it'd be preferable to hanging out with Vicki and upsetting Mum.

Dad didn't hit me that night when I got home. I guess Mum

must have read him the riot act. But he still didn't let off. One night a little while later he insisted on taking me out boxing with his mates. Afterwards, we went to one of their houses and Dad gave me something horrible to drink. When I tried to stand up, I fell over and couldn't get up again. Afterwards, my only memory was of lying on the ground, crying and hearing men laughing. I have no idea what happened.

It was around that time that Mum and Dad started arguing a lot. They'd shout at each other but then shut up whenever I came into the room. I didn't know what the matter was, but I knew that things weren't right. I'd always thought of our home as a place filled with love, but now hate had moved in and was taking over. I didn't like it but I couldn't do anything about it. Mum seemed really unhappy and often looked pale and unwell. She started spending more time in bed again.

Without Mum around so much to defend me, Dad started hitting me more, now using the buckle end of his belt. When he did it, it really felt as though I disgusted him somehow. Sometimes, when Mum was up, he'd even demand that she strap me. When that happened, if he wasn't in the room, she'd whack the side of the cupboard and tell me to cry out as though I was in pain.

One evening, Ronnie persuaded Mum to go out with him and his girlfriend Maggie for a drink at the Royal. Dad stayed behind and I could see him fuming that Mum had chosen to go out with Ronnie instead of him. When she returned a couple of hours later, he locked all the doors and refused to let her in. They had a blistering row either side of the front door that I'm sure the whole street heard. I raced to the back door, climbed on a chair and undid all the locks that had been put on to stop me going out when sleepwalking. I was enraged. How dare he do that to my mum! It was one thing being so horrible to me, but Mum didn't deserve that kind of treatment.

*

I'd always sensed that I was the odd one out in our family, with my skin tone and hair darker than Mum and Dad's, and that I was different to most of the other kids at school and in the neighbourhood. I had my bond with Brian and went dancing with my mates, but I still felt lonely and like I didn't really fit in.

Sometimes, I'd daydream that Dad wasn't really my dad, and that my real dad was someone kind and warm and thoughtful; someone like Jimmy Little. Maybe Mum wasn't my real mum, either. She didn't look like me, although Uncle Ken's wife Aunty Peg was darker. Perhaps Aunty Peg was my mum and she'd given me away ... My fevered imagination knew no bounds.

A couple of days after Dad had tried to lock her out of the house, Mum and I went to visit the relatives in Newtown. While I was playing with my cousins outside, I heard her talking in a hushed voice about Dad. I strained to hear what they were saying, but could only work out the odd mumbled word. Then Aunty Peg said in a very clear voice, 'Doesn't Dianne know who she is?'

My ears pricked up, but what on earth did she mean? Was I not really who I thought I was? I could feel my heart thudding in my chest as I waited for the answer. But Mum said something very softly and then the conversation moved on to other things.

On the way home, I could barely contain myself.

'Mum,' I said, 'I heard what Aunty Peg said.'

'Oh yes? What was that?'

She was either a wonderful actor, or had forgotten already. 'She asked if I knew who I was.'

'Oh, right, *that*,' Mum said. 'She was just being silly. She didn't mean anything by it.'

I was unconvinced. 'Mum, are you my real mum?'

She rolled her eyes. 'Dianne, of course I am! Now don't be silly. You just got the wrong end of the stick.'

I bit my tongue, but it didn't stop me wondering.

I'd received a bike for my birthday and I loved pedalling around the neighbourhood, usually with Lassie bounding after me. One of my favourite places to go was an old gypsy encampment in Clyde, a ten-minute ride away across Duck Creek. They seemed like interesting people with darker skin like me. They lived by the water, reading palms and telling people their futures. It was strange but I felt – or perhaps imagined – a real bond with them.

When I went over there with my friends and they had their palms read, I'd stay a little distance away. Afterwards, I was always able to tell them exactly what the gypsies had said. My mates thought it was amazing. But I'd always been psychic and, from a young age, Mum had been alarmed to hear me telling our neighbours what would happen to them later, and told me never to let on. She said if people found out, I'd be in danger of being sent to the Rathouse – her nickname for what was then the Parramatta Mental Hospital. I laughed and said it'd be a nice change from Parramatta Girls Home, that other place she routinely threatened me with.

I liked the gypsies. They were funny and friendly and had heaps of kids who'd all bundle in together. Their darker skin made me wonder if I was one of them. Perhaps I'd been taken from them and given to Mum and Dad. Perhaps I really did have five sisters and they all lived here in the camp. It was just one of my fantasies. Another favourite – for obvious reasons – was that I was the daughter of someone rich and famous and that one day they'd come back and claim me. Or maybe I was even the daughter of a notorious gangster, and that's why no one could tell me. Lenny McPherson was my godfather, after all. That felt thrilling too, but for different reasons.

I was spending more time alone, but my love of music never failed to soothe me. One record I played over and over again was Dusty Springfield's hit 'You Don't Own Me'. For some reason, I just loved the lyrics to that song. I didn't know why it had such strong appeal. Or why it annoyed Mum and Dad so much.

Chapter Five
The Pain of Loss

I turned fourteen in July 1960 but it was a gloomy affair. Mum had spent the past few weeks in bed, I was trying to avoid Dad, and Ronnie was off more and more with his girlfriend Maggie. She had a daughter named Trudi from a former boyfriend. Trudi was a year older than me and so often we'd be left together to either sit and listen to my records or given money to go to the pictures or to the pool.

Trudi was backward in some ways, but very forward in others. She worked for a living, she told me proudly the first time I met her. It turned out that Maggie took her fifteen-year-old daughter to the wharf when the ships came in. Trudi would go off with the sailors and *that's* how she earnt her money. I was shocked. If Mum had known what was going on and had been stronger, she would have put an immediate stop to it. I didn't dare raise the subject with Ronnie.

I longed for Mum to get better but I was scared she never would. One day, I overheard her telling my Uncle Ken that if anything happened to her, he was to take care of me. She also said my godmother in Parkes, Joy – whom I'd still never met – would be keen to take me too. Ronnie probably meant well, but he just stoked my fears when he said I shouldn't worry; Mum's will had been written by our local solicitor and apparently she was leaving everything to me, including her share of the house and all the money she'd saved for our trip to Parkes.

I didn't want any of it. I just wanted her to be well and happy again, and for my life to return to normal.

To cheer her up, I decided to buy her something nice. I'd saved my babysitting money and I went to the shops and saw a beautiful blue-and-white dinner service with a dragon motif. I loved it and I was sure Mum would love it too. I put it on lay-by and took on as much babysitting as I could manage to pay off a little bit more every week. The day of the final payment, I could barely sit still with excitement at school. I couldn't wait to surprise Mum with my special gift.

I nipped home first and, just as I was about to leave, Dad walked in with a strange smile on his face. He had a big parcel in his arms. He gave it to Mum, who was sitting on the sofa. I watched, transfixed, as she carefully unwrapped it ... to discover the same blue-and-white dinner service as I'd been paying for all those weeks! I looked at Dad, then at Mum beaming at him, then at Dad again. He winked at me and I raced to my bedroom and burst into tears. It turned out he'd gone and paid the balance of the lay-by and told

Mum the gift was from him. I tried to reason with myself that at least I'd seen her smile.

The only light in my life at that time was my first real boyfriend, Keith Morris. I'd met him at the milk bar and, although he was skinny, couldn't dance very well, was a Bodgie with greased-back hair and a quiff at the front and his family was worse off than mine, it felt to me, a lonely teenager longing for affection, like love at first sight. Even better, Keith was scared of no one, not even my dad, and would always stick up for me.

I'd found my knight in shining armour.

Keith's mum was wonderful, too. She must have recognised something needy in me, and tried to mother me as best she could. I really appreciated it. I think Mum was a bit jealous of all the time I spent at their house, but was probably relieved that they seemed like good people.

I took Keith home one day and we declared our intentions. 'We're going to get married and then we're going to both come and live with you, Mum!' I cried.

She laughed and shook her head. 'No, you will not! You can build a place of your own.'

'But I don't want to ever leave you. I want to live with you forever.'

'I'll come and visit you, love, don't worry. I'll always be here for you. But you're both still very young. Far too young to be thinking about marriage.'

She was right, and in so many ways. I soon found out, as lovely as he was, Keith also had a wild side and mixed with an older, rougher crowd. It wasn't long before he embarked on his first career: stealing cars. It was a choice of profession that would change the course of my life.

*

One hot afternoon in April 1961, Mum was sitting on the verandah and asked me if I'd noticed whether or not she'd taken her tablets. I said she hadn't, so she sent me off to the bedroom to fetch them. When I returned, she was lying crumpled on the ground, struggling to breathe.

'Dad!' I yelled. 'Dad, Mum's sick! She's collapsed! Come quick!'

I could hear the soundtrack from the TV game show *Pick a Box* coming from the lounge room, and the host, Bob Dyer, asking his catchphrase, 'The money or the box?'

'Dad!' I shouted again. 'Come now! It's Mum …'

'Yes, yes,' he called back. 'I'll be there in a minute.'

I heard Bob Dyer upping his offer of money to a contestant in lieu of opening the box, but no sound of Dad approaching. I started screaming as loudly as I could, but Dad still didn't come. Neither did anyone else. The street was empty.

In desperation, I put my arms under Mum's shoulders and started dragging her into the house, all the while calling for help. I managed to get her as far as the hallway and knelt beside her, trying to talk to her through my tears. Eventually, Dad came out, leant over, picked her up easily in his arms and carried her to the bedroom.

'I'll go and get Uncle Walter!' I shouted at Dad's back. He'd be in his caravan in the backyard and might know what to do.

At that, Dad turned on his heel. 'No, Dianne,' he said. 'I'll handle this.'

'But how about Aunty Peg?' I asked. 'We should tell her.'

'I've said no,' he snapped. 'I'll see to your mother.'

After what felt like an age, he came back out of the bedroom and phoned a doctor. It wasn't our regular family doctor who appeared, though; it was someone I'd never seen before. The strange man pronounced my mother dead at 6 p.m. on 11 April 1961.

I truly hated my father that night. Why hadn't he come when I called him? Why was he so unconcerned? Why didn't he let my uncle and aunt know what was happening? It was like he wanted Mum dead, as if he'd killed her.

I was inconsolable. My lovely mother was gone and I would never again feel her warm touch or see her beautiful face. The light had gone out in my world.

I went into the bedroom to say my final goodbye and saw her body move. For one glorious moment I thought maybe she was still alive and everyone had made a terrible mistake. But it was just gas in her body or her nerve endings dying, Ronnie told me later. She was icy cold to the touch.

Two undertakers arrived to take her away. I noticed, to my horror, that one had a cobweb on his coat and a little spider crawling on his collar. He looked like Boris Karloff, the horror movie actor I'd seen at the Crest Theatre. The undertakers were like a sight straight from hell. I told them they couldn't have her and tried to lock the bedroom door and barricade myself in. They easily overpowered me and dragged me to the kitchen. There, I picked up a knife from the bench and rushed at one of them. Dad stopped me and knocked it from my hand. I was so hysterical with grief, he held me down while the doctor injected me with something to calm me down. It took him two goes.

The undertakers took my mother away as I tried to run after their car. My legs felt like jelly from the shot I'd been given and collapsed under me. I lay sobbing on the road. Hearing the commotion, my uncle came out from the caravan, discovered what had happened and went mad at Dad for not telling anyone.

*

The next days were a blur. Our regular family doctor stopped by once and told me that Mum had had two leaking valves in her heart but she'd been too weak for an operation. She'd been hoping she'd last long enough to see me into adulthood. I wept afresh at that. Poor Mum; she'd been struggling to keep going just for me.

Even in death, she continued to help other people. She'd bequeathed her body to the university for research so medical students could be trained to help others.

But Dad still seemed utterly unmoved.

'It's the best thing she could do, giving her body to the university,' he said. 'It means I won't have to pay for her funeral.'

If I could have killed him there and then, I would have.

*

A few days after Mum's death, Uncle Ken phoned to say he'd take care of me. Dad hung up on him. Then my mystery godmother Joy turned up from Parkes to ask if she could take me to live with her. She looked nice, but Dad went mad at her.

'Get out of my house!' he bellowed. 'How dare you. Who'd look after me if Dianne went? She'll stay home and take care of me and the house.'

Ronnie stopped by and Dad sent him away with a flea in his ear, too. He wouldn't allow him to even step into the house and said he couldn't take any of Mum's stuff. He was forced to leave without even a single photo. Then Uncle Walter moved out of the caravan in the backyard, leaving us all alone.

I was terrified and hated Dad more than ever. I started spending more time at Keith's house, until Dad ordered me to get home and cook him his meals and clean up after him. I didn't dare disobey him. At night, I took to shoving a cabinet against my bedroom door so he wouldn't be able to get into my room – just in case.

Keith was sympathetic but in no position to help. His dad died soon after Mum and he went a bit crazy. He stole a car and went for a joyride and got caught. He ended up in Daruk Boys' Home in Windsor, an institution that later became notorious for its physical and sexual abuse. I think Keith was busy simply trying to survive.

Most nights I cried myself to sleep. I missed my mum terribly. Dad, however, didn't. He soon started writing letters to women in the lonely hearts columns in the newspaper. 'This one could be your new mother,' he'd say, pointing to a photo. 'Or this one.' Mum had only just died and already he was looking for another woman to take her place. I didn't want a new mum; I wanted mine back. I stayed holed up in my bedroom while he took out a succession of new women.

One night he came home late after an evening at the Royal accompanied by my brother's girlfriend, Maggie. They went into Mum's room and didn't come out till the following morning. I was horrified. Dad just laughed at the expression on my face.

I was confused and still grief-stricken and realised, yet again, that my father didn't care about me. Without Mum, and with Keith now locked up at Daruk, I had no one to look after and protect me. My blood brother Brian was moving out of Granville, Shirley was busy with her own boyfriend and all my old friends were growing up and drifting away. When you're in that kind of state, there are always going to be bad people out there who see vulnerability and pounce. One night I went to the pictures with two girlfriends and we were walking back home across a lonely paddock when a well-known neighbourhood thug suddenly appeared out of a side street. My two girlfriends saw him first and scattered. I was left alone.

He had a crazed look in his eyes but it was too late to flee and I tried to hold my ground and defend myself. He grabbed me and I fought back as hard as I could, trying to hit him and kick him in the shins and then bite him when his arms closed over my face. But while I'm sure my eyes went black and I zoned out on anger, I was still only fourteen and he was older and much heavier and stronger. He pushed me to the ground and lay down over me and ripped away my dress. He then forced himself into me. I was trying to scream but he'd squeezed all the breath out of me. When he was done, he zipped himself back up and sauntered off.

I was shocked and terrified and I limped home, shaking and smeared with blood and tears. My new red dress with its cross-over lace was torn and my white blouse was ripped. When I fell into the house, I started sobbing and immediately told Dad what had happened.

'You'll be right,' he said, barely looking at me. 'Take a hot bath with Epsom salts and I'll bring you something to drink.' He flicked on the TV. That was the end of the conversation.

A little while later he came into my room and gave me a glass of warm Guinness mixed with what tasted like salt and pepper. I tried to drink it but kept gagging. It was disgusting. I later found out it was a recipe for a home-made abortion.

Chapter Six
Easy Pickings

In the months following Mum's death, I didn't know which way to turn. Dad seemed unmoved, almost cheerful, and I just couldn't come to terms with how little he cared. In contrast, I was absolutely heartbroken, and his indifference only made the pain of loss harder to bear.

It was as if he somehow enjoyed my misery. He'd taunt me and goad me and needle me almost to breaking point. He'd tell me to cook him his tea, then he'd taste it and say it was disgusting, and knock the plate to the floor, or shovel the meal straight into the bin. He'd order me to tidy the house, purposely mess it all up, then say the house was dirty. I'd spend hours cleaning it, only for him to come home and tread mud all over the floor with his boots, spill food and drop tobacco everywhere as he rolled his smokes. He had to be doing all that deliberately.

In retrospect, I think he wanted me gone. With Mum out of the picture, he was free and didn't want to be bothered with a teenage daughter. And, in truth, I would have loved to have left – except I was underage and didn't have anywhere to go.

Most evenings, Dad would go out and stay out, sometimes all night. I assumed he was at the pub or out with one of the women he was always writing to. Whenever I ventured out during the day, I noticed the neighbours looking at me with concerned expressions on their faces. They must have thought it was terrible to see my dad out gallivanting so soon after his wife's death and were worried about me, a fourteen-year-old, left on her own in the house at night. I'm sure they talked about it, and everyone in the area soon knew ... but no one stepped in to help. In those days, people didn't interfere; they minded their own business. My boyfriend Keith was still locked up, so he couldn't help me, although his mum sometimes let me stay with her.

One night, I was asleep at home when a sudden noise woke me. I could hear boys' voices, and it sounded like they were right outside the house. I slipped quietly out of bed and carefully peered out under the curtain. A group of five or six boys were yelling and laughing. They tried to open the front door but it was locked so they went to the front windows to see if they could open them. I thought I recognised one of the boys from the pool. They'd obviously been drinking and I suppose were targeting the one house where they knew there were easy pickings.

I trod noiselessly down the passageway to Dad's room and opened the door a crack. It was empty. Although I felt panicky, I knew I had to stay calm. I tiptoed carefully through the house, trying not to make a sound, to the back door. I could see it was unlocked so, with my heart in my mouth, I shot the bolt. The sudden noise caught the boys' attention and they raced around the back.

I curled up into a ball on the floor as I heard them clatter up the three steps to the back door and start pounding on it. I could see the door shaking on its hinges with the force of their blows. They then turned to the windows and began hammering on the glass. I felt sure the glass would smash but, miraculously, it held. I knew it wouldn't keep them out forever, yet my legs were trembling too violently to allow me to get up and get to the phone to call the police for help. The boys were howling like animals. With a sick feeling in my stomach, I thought they sounded just like dogs on heat.

I was absolutely petrified. I'd been scared before – when I'd found Mum lying on the verandah, when the local thug had raped me, and when the two boys had jumped me before Brian came to my rescue – but this was different. This was pure, cold terror. In the other cases, I'd been able to do *something* to fight back against my attackers. This time, I had a bunch of blokes yelling outside my house and doing their damnedest to get in to do Lord knows what to me.

'We know you're in there!' they hollered. 'We're going to get you! We'll huff and we'll puff and we'll blow the doors down!'

They stopped as they fell about in hysterics, then started banging on the doors and windows again. I squeezed my eyes closed and pretended I was with Mum, watching TV or laughing over a silly joke. It didn't work.

'Come on, open up!' one of the boys yelled. 'We're losing

patience. If you don't open up, it'll be all the worse for you ...'

I could see his outline as he stood at the leadlight window in the front door, which was painted with beautiful red flowers that I'd always loved so much. I wondered how much longer it would hold. If they got in, I didn't think they'd be content with just raping me. They'd want blood. They'd torture me and might even kill me. I took a deep breath and summoned all my courage and shuffled into the lounge room to the telephone. With shaking fingers, I lifted the handset, grimacing as it pinged, and dialled the emergency number.

'I need the police!' I said when the operator answered. 'Now! Right now! Please tell them to come quickly. I think I'm going to be killed.' I gave her my address but didn't replace the handset in case the boys outside heard the noise. Just a few minutes later, to my relief, the sound of a police siren filled the air. A car screeched to a stop outside and I could hear footsteps racing away and others, heavier, marching up the four steps at the front of our house.

'Hello!' came a voice. 'Are you all right in there? This is the police. You're safe now. One of your neighbours called us.'

I don't know to this day how I reached the door so quickly but when I opened it I fell straight into the arms of a burly policeman. He held me gently till I'd stopped sobbing and then asked if I was okay. I nodded, unable to speak.

A policewoman stepped forward. 'How old are you, sweetie?'

'Fourteen,' I blubbered.

'And who lives here with you?'

'My dad.'

'And where is he now?'

'I don't know.'

The two officers steered me back into the house. The policewoman sat me down on the sofa while the man went into the kitchen and made us all a cup of tea.

'So does your dad often leave you here all on your own?' the policewoman asked me.

I nodded dumbly.

'And where's your mum?'

My eyes filled with tears again at the question. 'She's dead,' I said, hollowly. 'She died a couple of months ago.'

'Oh sweetie, I'm sorry to hear that. So could you tell me your name? And your dad's name?'

When Dad came home the following morning, he was ropeable. He'd been told by a mate that the police had been to the house and had knocked on our neighbours' doors asking them all how often a young girl was being left at home alone at night by her dad. He didn't appear to be at all worried that his daughter might have been attacked by a gang of marauding thugs; he seemed far more concerned that the incident might reflect badly on him. I couldn't help thinking that he might have told those boys I was home alone in the hope of finally getting shot of me.

*

A few weeks later I turned fifteen, but again, there wasn't much to celebrate. I quit school and went for an interview at the Arnott's Biscuits factory in Homebush, thirty minutes away by train. I lied and told them I was sixteen years old and they gave me a few shifts.

Even though I preferred learning at school to processing chocolate coating and packaging, I reasoned that if I didn't start looking after myself, no one else would. Dad wasn't giving me any money and I'd starve to death if I couldn't buy food. I kept up my babysitting, as I had Lassie's food to pay for too. Whenever I had some spare change I went to the local pool where I could swim in the silence underwater and try to forget my worries. I had no idea when Mum's will would be sorted out, but I knew, because Ronnie had told me, that she'd left her share of the house and her savings to me. I hoped that any inheritance I might receive would allow me to be a bit more independent.

In my spare time, I kept house for Dad, tidying, cleaning, washing his clothes and cooking his meals, but he still gave me nothing. The day he started making threats about strangling Mum's bird Clarrie, I phoned one of Mum's brothers and asked him to take her away. It was like losing another memory of Mum, but I didn't want to risk anything bad happening to her.

Dad was seeing another woman called Joyce and came home late pretty much every night. I know he was annoyed that he couldn't stay at her place in case the police showed up and wanted to check on me. I was nice to her – I was nice to all his women as I so craved older female company – but she didn't seem to like me. I got the feeling they both saw me as an irritation. I was in the way.

*

One evening I managed to slip out with some girlfriends to the ABC TV studios to watch the *Six O'Clock Rock* show again. I tied my hair in the same gauze ribbon I'd had on the day that Mum had seen me on TV. Dancing was another way of blocking out my problems for a couple of hours. On the train back to Granville, I thought I glimpsed the star of the show, Johnny O'Keefe, sitting in the same carriage. Of course I ran straight up to him. When he turned around, it wasn't him; it was a much older man. I went back to join the other girls but when we got off, the man started following us. I was nervous and went to the taxi rank to catch a taxi home instead of walking. The man followed me and must have overheard me telling the driver, through his open window, my address.

'Redfern Street?' he said to the driver. 'There's no such street as Redfern around here.'

I scrambled quickly into the cab. The driver looked at the man, trying to work out if we were together or not. 'Yes, there is, mate,' the driver said. 'You're obviously not from round here.'

'No, but it looks like a nice place with some nice girls,' the man said, looking straight at me.

To my relief, I could see the Harrison brothers approaching, and I started waving madly at them.

'Hi Di!' one of them said. 'Are you having trouble over here?'

'I don't know,' I said, staring at the man. He looked back at me, looked at them, and then took off.

'No, I think we're right,' I cried with relief. 'Thanks, boys.'

The next day, the very same man turned up at the house, asking for me. I was creeped out, but Dad seemed friendly with him. Over-friendly, even. He invited him inside and they had a drink together.

This man, it appeared, was Irish, just like Dad. They seemed more like old mates than strangers who'd just met. Dad called me into the lounge room.

'Dianne,' he said. 'Meet Colin O'Brien. He's interested in taking you out.'

'But ...' I started.

'No buts,' Dad said, looking at me thunderously. 'He's done the right thing, coming round to ask me if he can take you out, unlike that no-good loser Keith.'

'But Dad,' I whined, 'I don't want to go out with him.'

'Dianne, don't be so rude!' he snapped. 'He's a bit older than you, but I think he'll be good for you.'

And that was that. The deal had been done. I went on three dates with this Colin O'Brien, each one worse than the last. We went to the pub every time and he'd sit moodily over his beer and bourbon while I drank lemonade. He had little in the way of conversation and didn't even seem particularly interested in me. I thought he was lonely and tried to talk to him, but he was never very responsive. I think he just liked being in the company of a young and pretty girl, and was more interested in drinking himself into oblivion. At the end of the third date, when he was walking me home, I was chattering away about Elvis and Johnny O'Keefe and, without warning, he whacked me across my shoulder. It shocked me and shut me up.

I told Dad what happened when I got in, but he just shrugged and said I must have deserved it. Before each date, I'd pleaded with him not to make me go, but he wouldn't have a bar of it. He'd had no interest in any boyfriends before – apart from disliking Keith for standing up to him – but was adamant that I spend more time with Colin. I had no idea why ... until the day after the third date when Dad announced it was time to go away on holiday.

'Great!' I said, genuinely thrilled. I hadn't been on holidays for years. 'Where are we going?'

He sneered. 'Where are we going?' he mimicked me. 'Where are we going? Me and Joyce are going to the coast, but you're staying here.' He saw how downcast I was and laughed. 'But I'm not leaving you on your own,' he continued. 'No, I can't risk that. Not since you had the police round here, poking their noses in. I've arranged for your boyfriend to look after you.'

'Keith ...?' I asked, confused. 'But he's in lock-up.'

'No, you idiot, Colin. I've said he can stay in the caravan out the back. He can keep his eye on you. You cook his meals and look after him and he'll look after you.'

My heart sank. 'But I don't want ...'

'That's enough!' Dad shouted. 'I've had enough of your bleating. I'm doing my best for you here, but you're just so ungrateful.'

I tried a different tack. 'Maybe I could go and stay at Mrs Morris's? That way Colin won't have to come and stay here.'

'No!' Dad thundered. 'I've made all the arrangements. Now, get out of my sight.'

The day I stood at the window and watched Dad and Joyce drive off to the coast was one of the most miserable of my life. I felt abandoned and utterly alone – except for a creepy stranger living in the caravan out the back.

Chapter Seven
In Moral Danger

The first couple of days after Dad's departure were quiet. I worked shifts at the biscuit factory, and came home, cleaned up and cooked dinner. I left Colin's meal on the little table in his caravan then, despite Dad's orders, went to stay at Keith's mum's house for the night, making sure to leave before Colin got back from his job at the abattoir, and not to return before he left for work in the morning.

Colin was a good-looking man but he scared me. It was as if there was a deep anger simmering away under the surface, and it didn't take much for him to strike out. I'd discovered that to my cost on our third date when he'd hit me for no reason, and I had no interest in seeing that side of him ever again.

On the third evening, however, it was raining and I was late getting a taxi to Mrs Morris's place. I was just gathering my things when I heard the front gate click. I opened the door a crack to see who it was and, at first, couldn't see anyone. Then I looked at the verandah and Colin was lying there, drunk and dead to the world.

I was tempted to leave him there and go to Mrs Morris's house before he came to. But I felt sorry for him. The rain was beating down and he already looked soaked through. Besides, I reasoned, if anything happened to him, Dad might blame me. I went out into the wet, grabbed hold of the collar of his jacket and dragged him to the front door and then inside, just as I had when Mum collapsed four months before.

Colin was heavy, especially with wet clothes, and by the time I got him inside in the dry, I was panting. But I didn't want to hang around for him to wake up. I went to ring for a taxi and while I was waiting for the operator I heard a noise behind me, then a roar. I spun round and at the same time felt something heavy come down on my head. I fell to the ground and then smelled the sickly syrupy scent of cheap rum on my face. I opened my eyes to see Colin straddling me, pulling clumsily at my clothes.

'Colin!' I shouted. 'Get off me! Get off!'

He mumbled something I couldn't make out, pinned my arms under his knees and started yanking up my skirt. I tried to roll to one side, then the other, to get him off, but he only seemed to become more agitated.

'Colin!' I said sharply, thinking it might help sober him up and realise what he was doing.

'Shut the fuck up!' he shouted and belted me across my face.

I tried again to kick him and lift my shoulders from the ground, but he just readjusted his position. 'Stay still,' he barked, 'and this doesn't have to hurt.'

He then pulled down my underpants and raped me. And he was wrong. It did hurt.

When he'd finished, he rolled off me and lay back on the floor. I kept very still. I could taste blood and I ached all over. How could this have happened to me again? How could Dad have left me alone with this hateful man? I snuck a look at him, to where he was now snoring loudly, mouth wide open, saliva dribbling down his chin. I felt revulsion and then anger. I scrabbled to my feet, pulled down my skirt and, just as I noticed him stirring, raced out of the front door to one of my neighbours' homes, the one who'd called the police when those boys had been trying to break into the house. To my horror, I heard Colin stumbling behind me.

'She's mad! Mad!' he was yelling. 'I never done nothing to her. She's making it up.'

The neighbour opened her door. I quickly explained what had happened, and she looked from me – standing there with blood on my face and dripping down my legs – to him, shouting and swearing. Then she ushered me in, wrapped me in a blanket, slammed the door in his face and called the police.

Half an hour later, they arrived and arrested Colin on the spot. I could hear him screaming abuse at them, and at me. 'I didn't do nothing wrong!' he bellowed. 'She was asking for it. She's a little slut.'

That word again. I now had a better idea of what he meant.

With Colin safely under lock and key at the police station, I went home and cleaned myself up. Then I called a taxi and went to Mrs Morris's house. There was no way I was going to spend the night alone. She was horrified to hear of what had happened.

'Your father should be ashamed of himself, leaving his young daughter with a man like that,' she said. 'What was he thinking?'

I honestly had no idea.

*

Three weeks later, Dad returned from his holiday with Joyce and didn't say anything about Colin. I tried to tell him what had happened, but he wouldn't listen. I gave up. The police came round and asked why Colin was living in the caravan out the back, but I don't know what Dad told them. I did hear the police saying, though, that Colin had eventually admitted to raping me and was going to jail.

That night, I heard a noise outside my bedroom window and what sounded like a pebble striking the glass. I peeked out under the curtain and saw Keith standing there.

'Keith!' I exclaimed, opening the window. 'What are you doing here? Aren't you still ...?'

'Locked up?' he finished my sentence with a grin. His Bodgie quiff was gone and his hair was now shorn short. He looked a lot thinner and paler and older than when I'd last seen him. 'I've broken out. Can I come in?'

'Of course you can,' I said, opening the window wider so he could climb in.

He immediately hugged me close. It was so good to be held by someone I knew loved me, I felt tears spring to my eyes. I tried to get a grip. 'So how come you've broken out?' I asked.

'Mum told me what happened to you,' he said, pulling away and looking into my face. 'So I wanted to make sure you were all right. I was so worried. This is the only way I thought I could get to see you.'

I know it might sound weird now, but back then it felt like the most romantic thing I'd ever heard. 'But what if they catch you?' I asked. 'Won't you be in even more trouble?'

'Probably,' he replied nonchalantly. 'But I wanted to see you for myself.'

We stayed in my room for about an hour, talking quietly so we wouldn't disturb Dad. Then I suggested he go and sleep in Dad's car which I knew he left unlocked. Keith left the house the way he'd come in and I fell asleep, for the first time in a long time, with a smile on my face.

*

Next morning, I was cooking Dad's breakfast when he said I should cook extra. I looked at him quizzically. 'For Keith,' he added. 'I know he was here.'

'But how?'

'I heard he escaped from that home and a pot plant I had on the back seat of the car was broken. He must've slept there the night. Give him breakfast and then tell him to give himself up. He won't be able to evade the police for long. They're looking for him.'

When Dad left for work, Keith knocked softly on the front door and I let him in. I cooked him breakfast and told him what Dad had said. Keith said now he was out, he had no intention of going back again. But he needed some more clothes. Could I go over to his mum's and pick up some for him?

I didn't like lying to Mrs Morris as she'd always been so good to me, but I went round anyway and asked if I could have a few of Keith's clothes to wash for him. She wasn't fooled for a minute. She sent her other son George to follow me to find out where Keith was hiding. George saw us rendezvous in the park and then head to my house, and so he told his mum and she called the police. They turned up again and surrounded the house. I was so scared, I hid under the bed and didn't come out again until the police had re-arrested Keith, bundled him into a police van, and left.

I missed him even more after that. I was so touched that he'd been worried about me. He cared and seemed to be the only one. If only he hadn't stolen that stupid car. He might have still been around and Dad would never have been able to set me up with Colin. Because Dad definitely didn't care. Whenever I did something wrong and he beat me, I swear I could see hatred in his eyes.

I was almost relieved a couple of weeks later when Dad declared he was going on holiday again with Joyce. But this time, I think my neighbour must have tipped off the police, because a woman from welfare called round and caught me completely by surprise.

I was busy giving the house a thorough clean, as I'd been taught to do by Mum, and had taken up the rugs, hung them over the line and was beating the dust out of them. I'd decided to make it a more pleasurable task by wearing fancy dress: a pink fairy dress made of tulle that had always been a favourite. When I opened the door to her sharp rapping, I must have looked a real sight, dust all over me, the house in disarray and dressed in an outlandish frilly pink outfit. She said she'd come to see how I was managing after the rape, but must have made up her mind, on the spot, that I was an abandoned child and wasn't coping with being alone.

She insisted I come with her to Parramatta Police Station. I protested that I was quite all right, but she was having none of it. When we got to the station, the officers looked me up and down and I cursed my decision to wear such a bizarre outfit. 'It's fancy dress,' I said weakly, but I could tell they thought I was a mess and wasn't going to any parties. Then, as they did in those days, they told me I was considered a neglected child and someone exposed to 'moral danger', so I was effectively under arrest and wouldn't be allowed to go home on my own.

In fact, I wasn't to go home for the next thirty years.

At first, I was kept in the cells at the police station while they decided what they should do with me. I told them there was no one at home to look after Lassie and he might starve to death without me. But then my half-brother Ronnie found out that I was there and came to ask if he could take me away. The police refused and said he didn't have any rights of custody over me. I argued that they were mistaken; he was my half-brother and so must have some rights, but my pleas fell on deaf ears. Ronnie left, promising to go and collect Lassie. Dad called by when he returned from holiday too. I begged him to take me home but he just smiled in his nasty way.

'No, Dianne,' he said. 'You've been nothing but trouble to me. If you'd been sixteen years old, I would have thrown you out long ago.'

'But Dad, you don't really mean that,' I wheedled. 'Surely ...'

'Yes, I do mean it. Because you're still only fifteen, I couldn't, but now you've been taken off my hands anyway. Good luck.'

The following day, I was sent to the Metropolitan Girls' Shelter in Glebe. It was run by the Child Welfare Department as a home for girls awaiting hearings in the Children's Court. It was an old 1920s, two-storey building with a dormitory upstairs and a long, shared dining room table, with a laundry that the girls worked in with copper pipes you had to keep polishing. I hated it, but I kept my head down and just got on with the chores they gave me.

We all had a medical examination when we went in, and I was surprised to be called back into the matron's room the next day. She pulled no punches. 'You're pregnant,' she told me. 'Two months gone, we'd say.'

I gasped. Colin. The rape. I was having a baby. I didn't know whether to be horrified, or happy. I didn't know what to think. I wrote a letter to Keith and he wrote back immediately. He told me to say the baby was his, that we'd slept together the night when he escaped from Daruk Boys' Home. That way, they might let me go and live with his mum and he'd join us when he finally got out. It sounded like a great idea and I thought it was one Mum would have approved of too. So I told the matron Keith was the father and she noted it down in her big register.

Finally, the day came when I was to appear in Parramatta Children's Court. I was nervous, but the hearing was over almost as soon as it started. In those days, innocent children who were neglected and believed to be in moral danger were punished for it – even though their parents, or other supposedly responsible adults, were usually the ones who were to blame. It was an actual charge: being 'neglected, uncontrollable or exposed to moral danger'. Ludicrous, I know.

Dad was summoned to court to testify. He avoided my gaze, which worried me and, when called on to talk about my character, he painted a terrible picture of me. I didn't recognise it at all as the girl who'd kept his house, cooked for him, cleaned up after him and adored him until he started treating her with such offhanded cruelty. I think I listened with my mouth hanging open in shock. Then, at the end of it all, came the killer blow.

'Actually, I'd like to disown her,' Dad said to the judge.

I gasped and the judge frowned. 'Mr Westman,' he said coldly, 'you cannot disown an adopted child.'

What? I wondered if I'd heard right. *An adopted child?* Who, me? So I wasn't really Dad's daughter, or probably Mum's then, either? My beautiful mother wasn't who I'd thought she was? I sat there bewildered. But events moved on swiftly and the judge soon delivered his verdict. At age fifteen, I was sentenced to a spell in the dreaded Parramatta Girls Home – the place that Mum had jokingly threatened me with so many times in the past. She would never have dreamt, in a million years, that her words would come true.

As a policeman led me away, I walked right past Dad. 'So who's my mother?' I managed to get out.

He looked at me with absolute contempt. 'Oh, some bloody wog.'

Chapter Eight
Number 109

As we approached Parramatta Girls Home – a grim three-storey building by the river – I imagined I could feel a tide of misery and despair pulsing out from all the kids who'd been locked up there since the late 1880s. By the end of 1961 it was a truly dreadful place. Crazily, it catered for two entirely different groups of adolescent girls – those who'd been tried and convicted of some kind of crime, and those who'd simply been neglected, abandoned, orphaned or who were destitute and had nowhere else to go. Originally, the authorities intended to separate the two groups. But they soon discovered it would take more staff and money to run it that way. As a result, we were all lumped in together, both the girls who were classified as 'juvenile delinquents' and those who had done nothing wrong but had been the victims of abuse or neglect.

Can you think of any other place in the world today that would chuck both perpetrators and innocent victims in prison together? No, neither can I. It's astonishing now to think of young people being treated that way and being written off as immoral or criminal. Yet back then, we were left in no doubt at all of our position in society – we were rock bottom. It was obvious from the moment we crossed the threshold and were issued with our all-important numbers by which we'd be known from that moment on. And it was clear when we were searched by three male guards and told to strip and stand naked as they jeered and made crude comments. I kept my hand over my belly protectively, wanting to shield my baby from what felt like little more than a ritual exercise in humiliation.

'Get your arm down, number 109!' one of the guards snapped.

I glared at him, but he wasn't even looking at my face. He was looking everywhere but. 'Yes, sir,' I said meekly. Even at that early stage, I realised I had to pick my battles. I moved my hand and the guards looked me over. I'd been raped twice in my life, but their roving eyes felt like a third time.

The guard who yelled at me turned away, as if in disgust. 'Not a looker there among you,' he sneered. 'Now, into the showers!'

We shuffled off into the shower block where the guards continued watching us. There were no doors and no curtains and I noticed, with shock, that none of the toilet cubicles next to them had doors either. The guards tossed us towels and identical bundles of clothes: a cotton dress, a brown apron for working, a pair of socks and a pair of knickers.

'Get dressed now,' said another of the men. 'And hurry up. We haven't got all night.'

Next, the superintendent appeared and barked out the rules. There was to be no talking and no going anywhere in the building without permission. We were to get up at 6.30 a.m. sharp each day and perform our assigned tasks. Lights-out was at 9 p.m. each night, when we'd be locked in our dormitories. Punishment for misbehaviour would be severe. As I stood there, listening to his tirade, I felt my heart sink as low as it ever had. Mum had often playfully threatened me with this place but neither of us had any idea of how truly ghastly it was. If she'd have known, she never would have joked about it.

Nothing about Parramatta Girls Home felt real. I kept hoping that it was a nightmare and I'd soon wake up, wander into the kitchen and find my beloved mother making me breakfast. But this was my life now and I had to survive. I had no idea how long I was going to be here. Your sentence was a formal committal of six to nine months' 'training' but your release date was, in practice, left entirely to the super. Some girls, I found out, had been there for years. The super could choose to let you go, or keep you in, depending on what he thought of you ... or what you did for him.

Us new arrivals were marched up to the dormitory and each allocated one of the room's thirty thin mattresses. There was one toilet between the lot of us. I looked around and saw how bare it was; no other furniture and no knick-knacks, and dark iron bars on the windows that obscured any view of the world beyond. We'd been dumped here out of sight, out of mind, a bunch of kids no one knew what to do with. They'd decided to hide us away instead.

That night, I buried myself under my rough blanket and sobbed myself to sleep.

'Oh, Mum,' I whispered, 'how did this happen? It's only been five months and yet everything's gone wrong. I miss you so much. Why did you have to leave me?'

I thought about Dad and how he'd turned his back on me. I still suspected he'd told those boys I was alone in the house that time, and I wondered if he'd known what Colin O'Brien would do as soon as he got me alone. Well, Dad had succeeded all right. He had finally got rid of me.

I suddenly remembered the judge saying I was adopted. If that were the case, who were my real parents? Who was my *real* mother and might she still be alive? Why would she have given me away? Surely if she knew where I was now, she'd come back to rescue me.

I put my hand on my belly. 'Don't worry, bubba,' I cooed. 'I'll look after you. I'll never give you away. We'll be happy, you and me. When we get out of here we'll go live with Keith and his mum and Lassie. It'll be good, you'll see. I'll stick by you forever, and be a good mum to you, just like Mum was to me.'

Finally, I slept, exhausted by the day and the fear of what the days to come might bring.

*

The days and weeks in Parramatta Girls Home quickly began to blur. We endured a draconian regime, monotonous, hard and stinging with sadistic cruelty. The guards ruled their charges by fear. They were always conducting musters and body searches and making you strip in front of them, or open your towel on the way to the shower, sometimes rubbing their hands over your bodies. They said they were checking for marks or tattoos and there was nothing you could do to stop them. Every door in front of you and behind you was locked and unlocked by them, to remind you that you were never free. Our 'schooling' turned out to be laundry, kitchen duties, cleaning and maintenance – all so the Home could reduce its running costs – or being locked in a small room for hours with absolutely nothing to do. No sport, no games, no swimming, no relief at all. The guards said if we worked hard and were good – which we interpreted as doing anything, however awful, they asked us to – we might be rewarded with an outing. One day, someone said we were going to the swimming pool and my heart did a little flip of excitement at the thought of being in the water again, or even glimpsing the river which was so close by. But nothing ever came of it and I never met anyone who'd been granted an outing.

It was every girl's nightmare. We nicknamed the Home's doctor 'fish fingers' because he was always feeling us up. He would regularly 'examine' us by pushing a two-bladed speculum, known as a 'duckbill' because of its shape, into our vaginas and dilating it. He told us he did this to get a better view of our reproductive tract and make sure we were healthy and didn't have any venereal diseases.

We didn't believe him. Girls said he was checking for evidence of sexual activity and whether or not we were virgins. Those who were virgins would be passed on to the guards who'd sexually assault them. As if that weren't enough, other girls would be ordered to hurt them – or be punished themselves – or the doctor would get the thrill himself of personally breaking their hymens. Many of those girls later committed suicide. For the rest of us, the speculum felt like a torture or disciplinary device designed to hurt us and give the doctor and the guards watching sadistic pleasure. I couldn't imagine a more obscene way of making us suffer. I was also constantly terrified that they might hurt my baby.

Girls were repeatedly raped and sexually assaulted with broomsticks and bleach. To stop us telling anyone what was happening, our mail was censored. I wrote to Keith a couple of times, and wrote to Shirley and Brian too, but I was careful about what I said. I was grateful that Shirley wrote back, but I assumed it was just as hard for Keith to write as it was for me. You were only allowed visitors once a week but that didn't worry me so much; I only ever had one visitor, Keith's mum Mrs Morris, who came a couple of times and brought me biscuits and little treats. I tried not to cry, but she reminded me of the kindness of my own mum in my past life before everything fell apart.

The third time Mrs Morris came she was all business. She'd found out that I was pregnant and that I'd named Keith as the father.

'I know it must have seemed like a good idea at the time, Dianne dear,' she said. 'But I have to ask you, please tell them it wasn't Keith.'

'But ... but ...' I stumbled. I was confused. It *was* a good idea and, to be honest, the thought that one day I'd get out of here and go and live with Keith and his mum was about the only thing keeping me going. We'd be such a happy family together.

'I know it wasn't Keith,' she continued, looking pained. 'He told me nothing happened that time he escaped and came to see you. And I know that Colin raped you, so the baby will be his.' I must have looked heartbroken, because her voice softened and she reached out for my hand. 'The thing is, the police have been round to see Keith again. They're talking of charging him with carnal knowledge as you're both underage. At this rate, he'll never get out. And you don't want that, do you, dear?'

I shook my head glumly, my eyes filling with tears. 'No, Mrs Morris,' I said dutifully. 'I don't want that at all.'

'So I'm afraid you'll have to tell them it was Colin. I'm sorry, but there really is no other way.' She smiled encouragingly, then changed the subject. 'Did I tell you that Keith is due to come home just after Christmas? It's so exciting, isn't it? I can't wait.'

I went to see the super that afternoon and said I wanted to change my statement. A detective came round the next day and I told him with a heavy heart that Colin O'Brien was the real father of my baby. It wasn't the first time I cursed the day that Keith had decided to steal that stupid car and go for a joyride.

The detective was sympathetic and I think felt sorry for me. He told me he'd been to visit my dad and had tried to persuade him to come and take me home. Dad had refused point-blank. The detective shook his head. 'The way he was talking about you, it was as if you'd killed someone.'

'Well, he's not my real father,' I replied, as if that was somehow an excuse for him being such a bastard.

The detective raised his eyebrows. 'Yes, we're aware of that. We also asked him if he'd store your stuff in the back shed until you get of here but he said no. He said he'd burnt it all.'

I gasped. All the diaries I'd painstakingly filled with my thoughts, my dreams, my hopes growing up. All now just cinders. And my books, my clothes, my Elvis collection ... At that, I had another thought.

'What about Mum's ashes?' I asked hopefully. 'Can I have those?'

The detective had the grace to flush red. 'I don't think your father picked them up from the university. They disposed of them. And I'm sorry, I have more bad news for you. Apparently, your dad also had your dog put down.'

*

I worked hard at Parramatta Girls Home and didn't let anyone stand over me. I stuck up for others too. I always had something to say to anyone who tried to hurt another girl just for the fun of it. Mum had taught me to speak up for myself but I still don't know quite where I got my courage from.

One of the supers, Noel Greenaway, who was later jailed for twenty years after he was exposed by the Royal Commission, was an especially cruel man. He had a habit of calling girls up to his office and sexually assaulting them. One day, he summoned me. As I climbed the stone stairs, I felt sick and scared inside about what he might do. By the time I got there, I was almost crying.

'Stop blubbering, number 109!' he yelled.

'Yes, sir,' I replied, staring at the floor.

'This is for you. Look at it.'

I was terrified of what he might be doing, but then looked up. To my surprise, he was offering me a package. 'Well, take it then,' he barked. 'And get out of my sight.'

'Yes, sir,' I said, grabbing it from him and scrambling away so fast I nearly fell over my own feet.

Back in the dorm, I opened the package to find some pink rosary beads and a cross. It was a present from Keith's mum, Mrs Morris. I started to laugh with relief that I'd got out of the super's office unscathed. The other girls looked at me curiously. I was also touched that someone out there cared. I didn't know it at the time, but it was Mrs Morris's way of saying goodbye. She never came to see me again.

Chapter Nine
The Only Options

In some ways, I was lucky to be pregnant while I was at Parramatta Girls Home. Unlike many others, I was never raped, and I think that's because I was showing by now. Why choose a pregnant woman for your sex and power games when there were easier pickings on hand? If I lost the baby because of what the guards did to me, I imagined there might be trouble, too. I was also outspoken, so it was easier to pick on the weaker, more vulnerable girls.

One girl had been in for six months after stealing a pair of socks. Others, like me, were poor and had no one to look after them. Another girl arrived after her father stripped her naked, chained her to a tree and raped her repeatedly for three straight days and nights. Obviously, she was a complete mess, no doubt suffering terrible trauma. But she, and girls like her – often severely disturbed, mentally ill or with a physical disability – were either selected for 'special' attention, or were hurt by girls who were punished by the guards if they refused to obey orders to injure them.

Whenever any of the guards or other girls would pick on me, I always made sure I spoke up loudly and tried to look as if I wouldn't be intimidated. I don't know why they picked on me, but I knew I stood out somehow. I wasn't white, like most of the girls, but I wasn't black, either, like some of the others. I was just different. The Aboriginal girls got singled out for the worst treatment and I'd try to defend them. It was in my nature to stand up for the underdog, and they were definitely on the bottom of the pecking order.

*

One morning, I witnessed a girl being shoved into a big rubbish bin-sized bread bin. The guards then started kicking and smashing the bin with batons, sending the girl ricocheting from side to side. Once they'd had their fun and hauled her out, she had to be taken to hospital, a bloody, broken mess. We never saw her again and assumed that she'd died. Another lunchtime, I was told by a super to pour my bowl of slops over the head of a girl who wouldn't stop screaming. I refused, but then the super pushed me so I stumbled and dropped my bowl, so the girl got drenched, anyway. We'd be punished whether we did the guards' bidding or not.

If you did something wrong, or if the guards just felt like it, they might beat you with any weapon to hand – one day they smashed me in the face with a bunch of keys – or make you stand still for hours and bash you if you moved. You might be forced to clean the toilets and drains, stoke the furnace or scrub the concrete slab where we used to line up for visitors with a brush or even a toothbrush. I spent so long cleaning, polishing and then re-cleaning that slab, my knees were permanently damaged and have never really recovered. Other times, you'd be deprived of meals, put into solitary confinement, given sedatives and anti-psychotic drugs or – my personal horror – taken down to the basement, a pitch-black, vile place overrun by rats you could hear scurrying about but couldn't see. I swear there were ghosts down there too. This is where most of the rapes took place, far away from prying eyes, behind big heavy doors so no one could hear the screaming.

Many years later, in 2003 and 2004, some of us former 'Parra Girls' got together in a series of reunions which were covered by ABC TV. It opened people's eyes to a scandal many would never have dreamt possible. A decade later, in 2014, the Home was investigated by the Royal Commission. That was a huge relief to me and all the other women who had survived that evil place. It brought the memories flooding back, hearing of everyone's experiences. It was heartbreaking to learn of the toll it had taken on so many of the former inmates. Mental illness, suicides and suicide attempts, marriage breakdowns, health problems and self-harming were commonplace. Tragically, it was too late for many.

Seven of the ten people accused of harming us were dead by then, but at least Noel Greenaway got locked up. He was eighty-two when he was sentenced in 2020 to twenty years with a non-parole period of ten, so he'll probably die in prison. I for one hope he rots there. It might sound harsh, but when you think of all the beautiful young girls whose lives he crushed, he deserves it.

*

After six months or so in the Home, the abuse got so bad, and the crying and screaming at night so awful, that the girls rioted. We knew we couldn't win, but at least it drew attention to our plight and made the guards look bad. And when you've got nothing to lose, you'll do anything to try to find something to gain, however slight. A few of the tougher girls started shouting at the end of the mealtime, others joined in and then they all started to smash up everything they could lay their hands on. I stayed a little bit away as I wanted to keep my baby safe. It was terrifying. I saw a guard flogging a girl with a rubber hose, and then a whole host of girls climbed up onto the roof and started ripping up tiles and hurling them down at the guards below. The guards got out their pressure hoses and turned them straight on us.

While the riot was eventually quelled, it certainly had an impact. As a direct result, the authorities set up another home, the Hay Institution for Girls, as a maximum security annex for the more hardened girls. It's hard to believe but it was even worse than Parramatta. Girls weren't allowed to speak without permission, had to keep their eyes to the floor at all times, were forced to do hard labour like digging paths and breaking concrete, had hourly checks all through the night so they couldn't sleep, and if they disobeyed an order they were starved, locked in isolation and had their sentences lengthened. The Institution was in operation for thirteen long years.

Eventually, the Royal Commission was to hear of its barbaric crimes of rape, intimidation, bashings and druggings, too. Perhaps one day the surviving perpetrators will be brought to justice.

*

In November 1961, I was four months pregnant and thinking more and more about how I could see Keith when he finally got out. Del Shannon's 'Runaway' was top of the pops at the time and I remember singing it over and over to myself.

I worked hard at all my chores, tried to stay out of sight as much as I could, and began reporting feeling ill. At five months pregnant, I thought they'd be bound to give me some leeway, and I was right. Just before New Year's Eve, they agreed to transfer me to another home, St Anthony's, in Croydon. This one was run by nuns, the Sisters of St Joseph or 'Joeys' as they were known, and was a lot less regimented. Soon after my arrival, I began plotting my escape. Early one morning, when I should have been doing laundry, I slipped out the back and jumped the fence, walked for miles to the nearest train station and caught a train back to Granville. I went straight to Keith's house. By the time I arrived and rang the doorbell, I was exhausted.

Mrs Morris opened the door and visibly blanched. 'Dianne!' she said. 'What are you doing here? Aren't you still …?'

'I managed to escape,' I said. 'I had to see Keith.'

She hesitated, but just for a moment. 'Come in, come in,' she said, opening the door wider. 'You look so pale. In your state, you should be resting, not traipsing all over Sydney.'

I went in and sat down heavily at the table. 'I just wanted to see Keith. And you said he'd be home by now.'

She looked crestfallen. 'Unfortunately he got his dates wrong. He's not due home for another two months. He's not here, I'm afraid. Let me make you a cup of tea. I think we should probably tell the authorities. You don't want to have to spend any longer at that place than you need to …'

'Thanks, Mrs Morris,' I said. 'But I'm not going back. Can't I stay here till Keith gets out?'

She looked pained. 'No, that's not possible. He's meant to stay away from you ever since you said he was the father.'

'But I told the police he wasn't.'

'Yes, I know, but you still can't be together until you're both old enough. Now, let me call the police to take you back.'

I stood up. 'No. I'm not going. Tell Keith I tried to visit him.'

And with that, I walked out with a bravado I didn't really feel. I strode purposefully to the end of the street until I knew I'd be out of sight, and then wondered where on earth I could go next.

*

In the end, I went to a friend's place at Doonside, forty minutes by bus west of Granville, and she hid me for a couple of weeks. But I knew I couldn't stay out of sight forever. I would walk around the house singing the lyrics to 'Runaway' to myself to keep up my spirits. But it was an impossible situation.

Finally, I returned to Mrs Morris's and she gave me a big lunch, then called the cops. In one way, I was glad. I didn't have anywhere to go, or anyone who wanted me. It was almost a relief when that kind detective turned up again, although he said I'd now have to go back to Parramatta.

'But I don't think it'll be for long,' he consoled me. 'When you're seven months pregnant, you'll probably be sent to Myee Hostel in Arncliffe. That's where they send all the young unmarried girls in state care expecting babies. It's a much better place than Parra.'

Mrs Morris smiled encouragingly. 'That doesn't sound so bad, does it, Dianne?' She was obviously trying to gee me up. 'And then it won't be long before you have your baby. That will be wonderful, won't it?'

'Yes, Mrs Morris,' I said. 'And thank you for everything. Hopefully I'll see you soon with my baby.'

'Yes, of course, dear,' she said, hugging me. 'Good luck.'

I was only in Parra for another six weeks before I was transferred to Myee. It was indeed nicer, although it could hardly have been worse. It was more relaxed and we were actually taught things, like how to care for babies. I knew most of it already, though, from all my years of babysitting, and had a real flair for it. There was a toddler called Rex who also lived at the hostel. His mum was unmarried and had signed him over for adoption, but he kept going to couples, and then being returned again. He took a special shine to me and I looked after him most of the time I was there. He was a great kid. I couldn't believe his mum had let him go.

There were also a number of other kids there who'd been adopted out as babies but who were then discovered to have some kind of disability, so they were brought back, rejected. One afternoon, a shopping trolley was left outside the hostel with six-month-old twin girls in it, while a little boy, Stevie, whose mother had apparently had syphilis and who was severely disabled, lived in the hostel full-time. No one could go near Stevie as he growled and bit and seemed very fierce. But gradually I was able to win his trust and eventually he'd allow me to feed him and cuddle him. The matron was amazed.

One day, she took me aside. 'Now, Dianne, I need to talk to you about your baby,' she said.

I was puzzled. 'Everything's going fine. The doctor says I've only got a couple of weeks to go.'

'Yes, yes. But after the baby's born, what are you going to do?'

In truth, I'd been trying not to think that far ahead. I'd always had that fond notion of living with Keith and his mum, but I knew now that was unlikely to happen. The only other thing I could think of was trying to somehow get the Parkes money Mum had left me in her will.

'I'm not sure,' I said. 'I haven't thought ...'

'Well, let me help,' she said, kindly. 'Most of our unmarried mothers agree to give up their babies. Life is so hard on the outside for them. And a baby is a big, big responsibility. They want the best for their children, as I'm sure you do too, don't you?'

'Yes, of course,' I murmured.

'So we have lots of lovely married couples who are keen to adopt babies. They can give a child the very best start in life. They have nice homes and they really want a child. They have so much love to give.'

'But I don't want to give my baby away.'

'No, no, of course you don't,' the matron said. 'But you have to think of what's best for the child. What, honestly, do you have to offer him or her?'

I felt the tears starting and I bit my lip hard. 'I have all the love in the world,' I said, stubbornly. 'I'm going to be the best mum. No, I'm not going to give up my baby. I was adopted and look at me now. I have no one. I'm not going to let that happen to my baby. *Ever.*'

She let me go that day but returned to her theme over and over again.

A few days before I was due to be transferred to the Crown Street Women's Hospital in Surry Hills, back then the biggest maternity hospital in Sydney, the matron called me into her office again.

'Now, your baby . . .' she started.

'I'm not giving it up for adoption.'

'All right, Dianne,' she said, her voice colder now. 'You've made your point. But if you keep your baby, the way I see it, you have only two options.'

'What do you mean?'

'Well, you can come back here for a few weeks, but then you'll have to move on. And because you're a state ward, and unmarried, your baby will have to go into an orphanage until he or she is five years old.'

'What?' I gasped.

'Yes, you won't be able to keep your child here, and you don't have anywhere else to go.'

'But ... my baby ... in an orphanage ... That doesn't make sense. I'm the mother. My baby won't be an orphan.'

'But you're only fifteen, you don't have any fixed place of abode and no visible lawful means of support. When you turn eighteen, you'll no longer be a ward of the state and you'll be free to leave. So then you'll have two years to sort yourself out, find somewhere to live and a job, and then come back to the authorities and make an application to have your child back.'

'An application?' I repeated, dully.

'Yes, you'll have to prove you're a fit and proper person to look after a child.'

My brain felt like it was about to explode. 'But my baby won't even know me after five years! And then I bet it's bloody hard to prove you're good enough to get your baby back.'

'Don't swear, Dianne,' the matron said. 'But yes, you're right. It's not ideal. But then you do have a second option.'

'What's that?' I asked, feeling suddenly fearful.

She looked, for the first time, embarrassed. 'You could marry the father.'

That took a moment to sink in. And then it did. My chest tightened and I suddenly felt as though I couldn't breathe. 'Marry the father?' I asked, aghast. 'But he raped me! You're telling me I have to marry him to keep my baby?'

She looked down at her hands. 'Yes, that's right. I'm sorry, but marrying your rapist is your only option if you want to keep your baby.'

I felt the room swirling around me. Then I blacked out.

PART TWO
SEARCHING

Chapter Ten
Stealing Children

My baby was the most beautiful creature I'd ever seen. She was absolutely perfect, with long black hair right down to the nape of her neck. I fell in love the moment I saw her and vowed that, whatever happened, I would never allow her to be taken away from me.

'Hello, sweetheart!' I cooed when she was handed back to me after being bathed by the nurses. 'Lovely to meet you. I'm your mum. I'll always be your mum, you hear me? We'll never let anyone separate us.'

She was born on 13 June 1962, three weeks before my sixteenth birthday. I decided to call her after my favourite film star, Debbie Reynolds. I'd especially loved her movie *Bundle of Joy*, which I'd seen just before I was sent to Parramatta Girls Home. Its story about an unmarried girl who finds and takes care of an abandoned baby meant so much more now. My child would never be abandoned like the baby in the movie. She would be loved and cared for all her life.

Debbie was one of the few babies born every year with a 'veil' over her face – a portion of the birth membrane that was easily wiped off – but that was regarded as a good omen. The doctor who delivered her told me that it meant she'd be lucky all her life. I felt she was already proving lucky for me; she was giving me a reason to keep going.

So when the nurse appeared a few hours later flourishing adoption papers, I firmly shook my head.

'No, I'm keeping my baby,' I said in a much louder voice than I'd intended. 'No one or nothing is going to take her away from me.'

'*Really?*' the nurse asked, obviously surprised.

'Absolutely.'

The nurse looked flustered, and disappeared. She returned a few minutes later, trailing the matron. The matron scowled at me.

'Now, dear,' she said with a softness that belied her expression. 'The nurse here tells me you're refusing to sign the adoption papers.'

'Yes, that's right. I'm not going to adopt out my baby.'

'But it'll be hard for you. You're so young … you don't have a husband … and I've heard you have no family. We have some lovely couples who'll take good care of her.'

'No,' I repeated. 'She's mine. *I'm* going to take good care of her.'

'But you don't have anyone to help you,' she insisted.

'Well, I don't really know that,' I replied. 'I was adopted, but

I'm going to find my real family. In the meantime, I'm going to be the best mum she could ever need.'

'But are you *sure?*' the matron asked, now with a wheedling tone.

I nodded. 'I've never been more sure of anything in my life. This baby is my family. Debbie is the only family I have at the moment. And we'll always be together.'

I'd already taken as much care as I could to make sure she wouldn't be stolen from me. The nurses at Crown Street Women's Hospital were notorious for taking away the babies of unmarried teenage mums, despite their objections, and putting them up for adoption. Some of the girls at Myee Hostel told me they'd been held down after giving birth or pushed back in the bed with a crude wooden restraint board when they'd tried to see their babies.

They'd also warned me about the ways the nurses tried to trick them into signing adoption consent forms, telling them they were just signing forms to allow anaesthetics to be administered in case of a difficult birth. Only afterwards did they discover they'd actually signed adoption papers. They told me to make sure I didn't sign *anything* while I was in hospital, even if I was in agony during labour. I took their advice, kept my wits about me and stubbornly refused to sign a single document.

Unmarried women were considered inferior, second-class citizens, morally bankrupt, mentally unstable and unfit to raise children simply because we didn't have a husband. We were regarded as lesser people than the couples who couldn't have kids and wanted ours. I wondered if this is what had happened to my own birth mother. Had she given me up of her own free will, or had I been torn from her arms, kicking and screaming and pleading? The whole thing was ghastly. Look at my adoptive dad. Why would he have been a better person to raise me than my own mother?

*

Much later, in 2011 and 2012, an Australian Government Senate inquiry was held into how Crown Street ran this major adoption service, and how tens of thousands of young mums were forced to give up their children between the 1940s and 1970s, after being drugged, tricked, pressured or threatened to give their consent. The authorities called it 'forced adoption'. Some of the mums had a fiercer name for it – 'stolen babies', or 'stolen generation', similar to when Aboriginal parents had their children taken from them. In 2013, then prime minister Julia Gillard made a formal apology for the pain caused by the government's adoption policy at Crown Street and others around the country. She condemned the 'shameful practices' that had ruined the lives of so many mothers, and pledged more funding to help those women access mental health services and reunite with their children.

A few days after Debbie's birth, I was sent back to Myee. The girls I knew there surrounded us, hugging us both and congratulating me. I'd done incredibly well not having my baby taken off me, they said. How had I managed it? It must have been so tough when the authorities were well known for using every trick in the book. I smiled happily. I was just very, very determined, I told them.

While a few girls had managed to keep their babies, most hadn't. Some of them were drugged and just slept all day. Others sat dull-eyed and tearful, mourning the loss of their children. They nodded to me but I know I was a painful reminder of what might have been. It was an incredibly depressing place.

One bright spot was being reunited with little Stevie, who was still at the hostel and still growling at everyone. He was so excited to see me again, he wouldn't let me out of his sight and clung to me whenever he could. The poor little mite. He was desperate for affection and attention. You'd think, being among so many girls, he'd be mothered half to death. But so many were so distressed at losing their own babies, they couldn't risk becoming attached to another child. They knew it would mean only more heartache.

One girl, the others told me, had been working as a prostitute on the streets to earn money for herself and her baby when the cops picked her up one night, discovered she was only fourteen, and brought her to Myee. They contacted her mum who lived in the US and she flew out to collect her. When she arrived, however, she refused to take the baby. As a result, the baby was adopted out and the night before her mum came to pick her up, the girl just vanished. The rumour was she was so heartbroken and felt so betrayed she refused to see her mum and ended up back on the streets.

Another girl who came in while pregnant was just saying hello to us all when she stopped dead in her tracks. She then ran over to a little boy who'd just come back to the hostel from being fostered and started hugging him and weeping that he was the baby she'd been forced to give up when she was fifteen, three years earlier. The matron prised her arms away from the terrified kid and phoned social welfare, telling them that she couldn't stay.

I talked to all the girls, listened to their sad stories and tried to advise them the best I could. Instinctively, I wanted to help the underdogs. Of course, I was an underdog too, but I was a lot luckier than some. I had Debbie, my smiling, chuckling little bundle of joy. But the matron's threat that I'd have to marry Colin O'Brien if I wanted to keep her still haunted me.

One night, when everyone was asleep, I went down to the nursery to feed Debbie. Another girl, Bev, came with me to feed her baby, which was always in the crib next to mine. I liked Bev a lot. She was Aboriginal, she told me, and she wasn't married either, and was sparky and funny and bright.

'You know,' she said, as we reached the door of the nursery, 'I don't like this hole. Do you fancy getting out? Let's run away.'

I looked at her, amazed. Run away with our babies? But the more I thought about it, the better the idea seemed. If I could get away, there's no way they'd be able to force me to marry my rapist. Debbie and I would be free. The last two times I'd run away – from home when Mum was still alive, and then from St Anthony's – hadn't worked out too well, of course, and I'd ended up back where I started.

But this time I'd be with Debbie. This time it'd be different.

'All right,' I said to Bev, brimming with enthusiasm. 'I'm game if you are.'

Bev grinned. 'Okay, but we'd better hurry before anyone else comes down.'

We darted into the nursery, picked up our babies in their cribs next to each other and made for the back door. Thankfully, it was unlocked, and neither baby made a sound as we slipped quietly through. Then we ran and ran and ran through the dark night, as fast as we possibly could. After twenty minutes or so, we slowed to walking pace to catch our breath. Neither baby had cried or even stirred, so we congratulated ourselves on the success of our plan.

'What now?' I asked Bev.

'Let's go to the station,' she said. 'It's not far and we could keep to the backstreets.'

We walked for another thirty minutes or so, winding our way through the suburb, fearful someone might have noticed our absence and be coming after us.

But when we arrived at the station, we were stymied. Of course! There were no trains at night. We'd have to wait at the station until it opened in the morning. Bev was from Newcastle, about 120 kilometres north of Sydney, and wanted to get back there. I'd intended to go to Granville, although it suddenly occurred to me that I had nowhere to go there, and no one who wanted to see me.

'How about we walk down to the river and camp there?' I suggested. I knew the Cooks River was close by and I had this sudden urge to be by water.

Bev looked at me as if I were mad. 'That's a long way to walk with our babies.'

I shrugged. I thought it'd be worth it. 'What do you think, Debbie?' I asked, opening her blanket for the first time to see if she was awake. The baby looked back at me quizzically. And I looked back at her. Shit! This wasn't my baby! I'd picked up the wrong one! The nurse must have moved her crib. 'Oh my God, Bev!' I shouted, making both her and the baby in my arms jump. 'I've got the wrong baby! This isn't Debbie! I don't know who it is!'

Bev peered at the baby in my arms. 'Bloody hell! That's Trish's baby. She does look a bit like yours but under that blanket, who could tell?'

I was dumbstruck. I'd struggled so hard to keep Debbie, battling so hard to stop her being taken away from me, and here I was, stealing someone else's baby from them. I'd have to get back before it was discovered.

'Bev, have a look at your baby,' I urged her, wondering if she'd picked up the wrong one too.

She gingerly opened the bundle in her arms and smiled with relief.

'That's great,' I said. 'But I'm sorry, Bev. I've got to go back.'

'Of course. But I'll come back with you. I don't fancy sitting out here all night on my own, and maybe it wasn't such a good idea, after all. If we get caught, who knows what might happen?'

We looked at each other, knowing we were both thinking the same thing. We couldn't risk giving the authorities any reason to take our babies away. It's the fear of all state wards: knowing you have so little control over your lives.

'Let's go,' I said. 'With a bit of luck, no one will know that we ever left.'

We ran back almost all the way to the hostel, snuck in the back door, and I put the baby I'd taken back down in her crib while Bev sat down to feed hers. I then found Debbie and gathered her up in my arms.

'Oh, I'm so sorry,' I whispered to her. 'I keep saying we'll never be apart and then I try to run off without you. I promise I won't ever leave you again.'

A nurse came in and smiled to see us both sitting there. 'Good girls,' she said. 'Well done.'

She really had no idea.

Chapter Eleven
A Terrible Choice

My days at Myee were fast running out. I had my sixteenth birthday in there in July 1962 and was told by the matron that my stay was up in two weeks' time. I had to make my decision. If I refused to give Debbie up for adoption, she said, I had two choices. I could let her go into the orphanage in Frenchs Forest, around 30 kilometres away, for the next five years. Or I could marry her father. It didn't feel like much of a choice to me. Losing her for five years would seem like a lifetime. But the thought of marrying Colin O'Brien, the man who'd raped me after smashing me over the back of the head, made me feel sick.

One day, the matron told me that Colin's mother, Mrs O'Brien, wanted to come and see me at the hostel and meet her grandchild. I said I'd think about it.

'But Dianne, you should meet her,' the matron said. 'She might be nicer than her son, and it sounds as if her family has money. They'd be able to take care of you and Debbie. Just think about your daughter.'

'I am thinking about my daughter!' I cried. 'I think of no one else. But a man who could do that to me. What kind of father would he be?'

'Mrs O'Brien has said you'll be living with her and her husband, as well as their son. So you won't be alone with him. And his spell in jail might well have knocked some sense into him. She says he's very sorry for what he did.'

'Where do they live?' I asked, sullenly.

'A place called Cobar.'

I looked blank. I'd never heard of it.

'It's in the far west of NSW, about 750 kilometres north-west of Sydney in the outback. It's an old mining town. It'd be a nice change for you, and lovely for Debbie to grow up in the country.'

'Geez, that's a long way away.'

'Yes, I know,' she said and smiled encouragingly. 'But it'll be a fresh start. Think of it like that.'

*

Eventually, I agreed that Mrs O'Brien could come and visit us. She was warm and friendly to me, and went to pieces over Debbie.

'She's absolutely gorgeous, dear,' she said. 'Please come and live with us. We'd be delighted to have you. And Colin ... I think he's grown up a lot. He'd be so excited to see his daughter.'

I looked at her sharply.

'And you,' she said quickly, a little too quickly.

The matron was delighted at how well our meeting had gone. When Mrs O'Brien left, she called me back into her office. 'She seemed very nice, didn't she?' she said. 'What did you think?'

'Yes, she was nice. And she seemed to really take a liking to Debbie.'

The matron nodded. 'Apparently they have a lovely house in Cobar.' She paused for a moment. 'So what do you say? Are you prepared to marry her son and take Debbie up there to live with them?'

I looked down at my hands. It was a choice between two terrible things. 'Honestly, I don't seem to have any other option. I have a bad feeling about it, and my instincts are usually right. But what else can I do?'

'Yes, I'm sorry, but it does seem like the best path. And on the bright side, you'll be off the department of social welfare's books, so you'll be a lot freer, and, if worst comes to worst, you could always run away. At least social welfare won't be chasing you.'

I grimaced. Run away. I liked the idea of that, but it hadn't worked in the past, so why would it work in the future? I shrugged.

'Okay,' I said. 'I'll marry him. But I'm only doing it for the sake of my daughter.'

Two days later, I packed my few possessions, put Debbie in a little pink romper suit, said a sad goodbye to Stevie and promised I'd see him again, and went with one of the hostel staff to a house in Cabramatta owned by Colin's friends. From there, a few days later, I'd be picked up for my wedding, I was told. His friends, Mr and Mrs Horsfield, turned out to be lovely, a gentle older couple who welcomed me into their home as if I were long-lost family. The next morning, I asked if they could watch over Debbie while I nipped out for a bit. They said it would be their pleasure.

The first person I went to see was the solicitor Ronnie had told me about who'd written Mum's will. This was my carefully plotted Plan B. I'd pick up my inheritance and hide it away so, if I did decide to run away from Colin and his family, at least I'd have plenty of money to keep myself and Debbie.

I caught the train back to Granville, went to the solicitor's office and explained who I was. He looked up Mum's file and confirmed she'd left me a large sum of money. Then he frowned. He was sorry, but the money had already been paid into a bank account. I said that was impossible; I didn't even have a bank account and I'd never received a penny. He looked at me over the desk and again said he was sorry. There was nothing more he could do.

I gathered my wits about me, thanked him and walked out. I was bewildered. What on earth was going on? The next person I went to see was Mum's nephew, Uncle Ken. I asked him if he knew anything about it. And he did.

He'd heard Dad had come up with an elaborate ruse to access the money, and had taken it all for himself. It was like I'd been given an electric shock. My head hurt and I could feel a sharp pain in my stomach. I could hardly believe it. Dad had cheated me out of my inheritance. How long had he been planning this?

I felt sick. All the money Mum had been carefully collecting for me all those years, all the times she'd gone without, all that scrimping and saving, had been for nothing. Well, not for nothing, I suppose. Dad had obviously benefited.

I decided to go to our old house and confront him. It wasn't just me who was going to suffer now; I had my daughter to look after. I summoned all my courage and marched down to Redfern Street. By the time I got to the front door, I felt my bravado start to wane, but I knocked quickly before I could change my mind. I could hear footsteps approach and then the door opened just a crack. I saw Dad's face peering out.

'Hello,' I said. 'It's me, Dianne. Can I come in?'

He opened the door a little wider and looked me up and down. 'No,' he said. 'You're not welcome here.'

'But Dad ...'

I heard another voice, a woman's voice, in the background. 'Who is it, George?'

Dad turned and shouted back, 'No one! They're just leaving.'

He obviously hadn't waited long to move his next woman in. But *no one*? I was his only child. It felt so strange being on this side of the door, and stranger still to see Dad standing where my mum should have been. 'Dad, you have a granddaughter now, Debbie. Don't you want to meet her?'

'No,' he snapped and went to shut the door. I was quicker than him. I got my foot in before he could push it closed.

'Well, okay, but what about my money?'

'What money? I don't know about any money.'

'The money Mum left me. You know. The money she'd been saving up for me.'

He shook his head. 'No, there's no money. Now get your foot out of the door before I break it.'

With that, he kicked my foot out and slammed the door. I turned and walked down the path, and then down the street. I looked back only once, and could see him standing by the front gate watching me, presumably to make sure I was really leaving.

As I walked, I cursed him. He was a hateful, hateful man. My lovely mum, the woman who'd devoted her life to him ... he hadn't even bothered to pick up her ashes and now he'd swindled both her and me. I was glad he didn't want to see Debbie. She was going to have nothing to do with her grandfather. I wanted to protect her against such evil.

On the way back to the station, I bumped into my old friend Shirley. She was pleased to see me, and asked me how I'd been. Everyone had been so upset when they'd heard I'd been sent to Parramatta Girls Home, she said, but she'd kept them updated via our letters. Brian asked after me regularly, too. I told her I had a daughter now, a beautiful little girl called Debbie. She asked me if my old boyfriend Keith was the father. I shook my head; it was someone she didn't know, I told her. She congratulated me and told me Keith had been released from the boys' home and had been running around with a few other girls before he got into another spot of bother and had been sent away again. My heart sank. So, my Plan A wasn't likely to work, either. It sounded like Keith was well and truly over me – and still had an appetite for trouble.

'But his mum's hoping he'll be out in another six weeks,' Shirley said.

It was a sliver of information I stored away in case I might need it in future.

When I got back to Cabramatta, the old couple said Debbie had been the perfect baby, and they'd loved looking after her. I thanked them. They were so sweet, I hoped that, with friends like these, maybe Colin wouldn't be as bad as I imagined.

*

The next morning, Mrs Horsfield asked me what I planned to wear to my wedding. I said I had no idea, I hadn't really thought about it.

'But it's only five days away,' she pointed out. 'Do you have anything you could wear?'

I only had two dresses and neither was particularly smart. I'd put on so much weight during my pregnancy, too, and it was taking a while to go.

'Not really,' I told her. 'And I don't have any money to buy one.'

'Come and look in my wardrobe,' she said. 'We might find something in there that will fit you.'

In truth, I didn't care what I was going to wear. I know most girls are excited at the prospect of their wedding day and want to look their very best. But to me, this wedding was little more than a sham, a marriage of convenience to someone I felt I already loathed. But Mrs Horsfield was insistent and I dutifully stood and watched as she went through her wardrobe.

She raked through her dresses until she came across a hideous green number. 'This might fit you,' she said, holding it up against me. 'And it would be nice as Colin is Irish and green is the colour of Ireland, and you said your mum was Irish, too. Why don't you try it on?'

I nodded. I thought the dress was awful, far too old for me and horribly frumpy, but it was kind of Mrs Horsfield to try to help. I slipped into it and immediately felt itchy from the rough cotton.

'Yes, that looks … all right,' Mrs Horsfield said, turning me towards the mirror. 'What do you think?'

I thought I'd never looked worse, but I didn't want to hurt her feelings. Besides, who cared what I looked like on my wedding day? I certainly didn't. 'That's lovely, thank you so much,' I said. 'That'll be great.'

*

That night, I was fast asleep when I woke suddenly at a commotion in the house. I checked Debbie was still in her cot, then padded quietly to my bedroom door. I could hear screaming, shouting and swearing, and then a thunderous crash. I opened my door, went onto the landing and looked in through the open door of Mr and Mrs Horsfield's bedroom.

And there was Colin O'Brien, larger than life and punching old Mr Horsfield and pushing his wife around. The crash looked like it had been Mrs Horsfield falling onto the wardrobe. Colin looked up, saw me and roared. I'd heard that sound before.

I darted back into my room and tried to shut the door against him, but he wrested it from my hand. I then stood protectively in front of Debbie's cot.

'Get out of my way!' he yelled. I could smell the drink on him. 'I want to see my daughter!'

He grabbed the cot and I did too. Debbie woke up and started crying. We had a strange kind of tug-of-war until he finally let go, swore at me and lumbered off. All I could hear was Debbie crying and Mrs Horsfield screaming. I tried to calm Debbie down, then went out to see if I could help the old couple. But Colin was still there and he grabbed me and dragged me into the laundry. He held me by the neck over the sink, trying to strangle me. I could see rage in his eyes. I struggled and struggled, kicking his shins and then aiming my heel at his crotch in the way the Harrisons had taught me. But I could feel the breath being slowly squeezed out of me. I was sure I was a goner.

Then I heard the sound of the front door opening and the thunder of heavy footsteps and felt his grip on me loosen. Mrs Horsfield, bless her, had phoned the police. A policeman pulled Colin off me and, with the help of another, handcuffed him and took him away. I rushed to Debbie to check she was all right, and then brought her into the lounge room where a nice policewoman sat me, and the old couple, down.

Mr and Mrs Horsfield were clearly shaken but said they didn't want to press charges.

'Do you know that brute?' the policewoman asked me.

'Yes,' I whispered.

'Who is he?'

'He's Colin O'Brien. My fiancé.'

'*Your fiancé?*' she asked, incredulous.

'Yes,' I replied. 'We're due to get married in four days.'

'Well, you won't be now,' she said. 'Now you know what he's really like. You'd be mad to marry him.'

'But I'm going to,' I said.

She stared at me like she couldn't believe her ears. 'Marry him and you'll have a life of misery.'

I looked down at Debbie in my arms and then back up at the policewoman. She didn't know I had no say in the matter, that I was doing it for my daughter. I tried to smile bravely, but my heart was pounding. 'Yes, I think you could be right,' I said.

Chapter Twelve
Married to a Monster

Sunday, 12 August 1962 was one of the most miserable days of my life. When I walked down the aisle in that terrible prickly green dress and saw Colin O'Brien standing at the altar in an ill-fitting suit he'd borrowed for the occasion it was as much as I could do to not turn on my heel and flee. Thankfully, he appeared to be sober and was quiet and well-behaved. It was as though nothing had ever happened. When we began reciting our vows, we barely looked at each other, but when he pledged 'Till death do us part', I couldn't help sneaking a glance at his face. It was blank.

None of my family was there, and Colin's parents were waiting for us in Cobar, so there were hardly any of his there, either. Mr and Mrs Horsfield turned up to hold Debbie and, I suspect, to support me, for which I was extremely grateful. The handful of other people might have been Colin's friends, but he didn't introduce us so I had no idea. The big brick Catholic church, Sacred Heart Cabramatta, was only eight months old and, with such a measly gathering for a wedding, I bet the parish priest Father Darcy O'Keefe found it miserable, too.

After the ceremony, we went back to the Horsfields, where I went to my room with Debbie. Colin slept in the front room. I was feeling feverish and had a splitting headache and went straight to bed. The next morning, I was feeling even worse and my face looked odd in the mirror, like it was swollen. But we got up early, I said a sad goodbye to the kind couple, and we caught a taxi to Central Station for the first part of our journey to Cobar. As I watched Sydney slip by out of the carriage window, I held Debbie tight in my arms. My search for my real parents would just have to wait till I got back to the city. I had no idea what kind of life was waiting for us in the country, but I had to try – at the start, at least – to make the best of it.

'Are you hungry?' I asked Colin. 'The Horsfields made us some sandwiches.'

'Yes, great, thanks,' he said.

I'd lost my appetite and the headache was back again. I felt tired and miserable. The train ride to our first stop, Dubbo, was going to be a long one, Colin warned me. I said a quiet goodbye to Granville when we rattled past and wondered if I was travelling further and further away from my real birth parents. Then we went through Parramatta, then Penrith and climbed steadily into the Blue Mountains, west of Sydney. I gazed out at the steep slopes in the distance, the green chasms and the spectacular views.

I hoped one day that I'd see them properly for myself.

As the train started descending, my ears popped with the pressure and we headed past the old mining town of Lithgow, then Rydal, Bathurst ... Debbie slept most of the way, lulled by the gentle rocking of the train, and I fed her whenever she woke. Colin gave me a bottle of water. Blayney, Millthorpe, Orange ... it felt as though the journey would never end.

Finally, after some five hours, we arrived in Dubbo, picked up our stuff, and then found the Broken Hill coach that would take us to Cobar. We stopped in Narromine, Trangie, the weirdly – and quite wrongly – named Nevertire, and then Nyngan, where I caught my first glimpse of the mighty Darling River as we crossed over its tributary the Bogan. I was feeling quite ill by now, but the river lifted my spirits and I wondered if it went out all the way to Cobar. I hoped it might. The matron had told me the O'Briens had a lovely house and I fell asleep dreaming of a cream-stoned castle on the banks of a sapphire river, framed by mighty red gums and pale grey coolabahs, with trailing willows and the bright yellow blossoms of silver wattle.

I felt a hand shaking my shoulder and opened my eyes. It was just Colin and he was telling me to wake up. I rubbed my eyes, gathered Debbie and my belongings and climbed down from the coach. All I could see was dust. My heart sank. It was nothing like my rosy vision of the place. But there was Mrs O'Brien waiting to meet us, and I smiled in greeting. She looked straight past me to Debbie in my arms.

*

I hadn't really left the big city since I'd moved to Sydney from Parkes at age three, so I knew Cobar would be a shock, but I wasn't expecting anything like this. The O'Briens' house wasn't a castle on the river, but a plain brick building on a dull suburban street. The town didn't even look like a town. It was an old mining settlement on a dusty flat, founded on what was once the biggest copper mine in Australia and the promise of gold nearby. It had some beautiful big old buildings from its glory days in the late 1800s, like the Great Western Hotel, with what locals said was the longest verandah in NSW, and the old Cobar Post Office and court house. But the mines had mostly closed, people had lost their jobs and many had moved away as a result. Cobar's population was now around 2000, a fifth of what it had been at its peak. By the time we arrived in 1962, the place had a real air of desolation. There was a bit of sheep farming, but unlike my beautifully green Parkes to the south-east, there was little rainfall and the soil was dry and hard and a dull orange colour. A lot of the trees had been chopped down for the early miners' huts and, as a result, the town was always dusty. Even worse, there was no river. The Darling was the closest – but it was 160 kilometres away, at Bourke to the north. Cobar was in the middle of nowhere, surrounded by the vast outback whichever way you turned.

I felt trapped, but then I didn't have anywhere else to go, or the means to get there. Not only that, I was diagnosed with mumps, which explained why I'd felt so rotten on the trip out from Sydney. I decided I'd better just toughen up and get on with it.

Colin and I moved into his old bedroom in his parents' house, which I didn't mind at all. I thought if he started drinking again and got violent with me, they'd be there to protect me and Debbie. While Mrs O'Brien doted on my daughter, she blew hot and cold with me and you never quite knew where you stood. Mr O'Brien acted the same. He barely said a word. The only bright spot was Colin's sister Sue, who I liked immediately. She lived nearby but was a bit of a mess. Her husband had left her for another woman and most of the time she was in tears. She wasn't coping at all.

Colin went out to work every day, doing some stuff at one of the remaining mines, which I was thankful for. But it did mean I was left alone with his mum. On the second day, she laid down the rules of her house.

'You can do your washing, boiling the nappies in the copper and everything, on Mondays and Tuesdays,' she said firmly. 'The rest of the days are mine for the laundry.'

'Thank you, Mrs O'Brien,' I said, 'but with a baby, I need to do the washing more often than that. Otherwise, the dirty nappies will stink the house out.'

She scowled. 'No, Mondays and Tuesdays are yours. If you're going to live in my house, you have to obey my rules.'

'But it doesn't make any sense, I need to be able to wash more days than that.'

'Now, look here, young lady,' she said. 'I don't want any of your cheek. We're looking after you and your daughter out of the goodness of our hearts, so you don't fall back in the gutter where we found you.'

I felt my temper rise, but knew I had to control it. Mum had brought me up well, she'd taught me how to keep house and look after myself, and it angered me to hear any slight that I thought anyone might be making against her. 'No, Mrs O'Brien,' I said as calmly as I could manage, 'you didn't find me in the gutter. I was living at home until your son … your son …' I didn't know how to finish the sentence.

She looked at me coldly. 'What's in the past should stay in the past,' she snapped. 'Now, we're talking about wash days. I've told you when yours will be. That's the end of it.'

I tried to do as she'd asked me for the first week, but the dirty nappies soon started piling up. So one day – a Friday I think it was – I snuck into the laundry.

Mrs O'Brien came home unexpectedly early and caught me. 'You should learn to do what you're told!' she shouted. 'I told you that you couldn't boil the nappies on a Friday. Why did you disobey me? Get to your room!'

Mrs O'Brien only seemed interested in Debbie, and I got the feeling that I was just someone to be tolerated, an irritant who was getting in the way between her and her grandchild. She was so cold and hard; I'd never met another woman like her. She often picked up Debbie and took her to the sitting room or out on the verandah, and I'd trudge behind them, watching them together, like a shadow. I didn't trust her, but she never showed any signs she would ever hurt Debbie. She adored her, while her son had no interest in his daughter at all. Occasionally, when I knew Mrs O'Brien was looking after Debbie and didn't want to be bothered,

I'd slip out to the local swimming pool for some blessed relief in the cool, calming water.

That night, when Colin came home from work after stopping off at the pub on the way, he yelled at me too for not keeping the room tidy enough. It was hard with a small baby, but he didn't seem to realise that. There were clothes and nappies and toys and bibs and baby blankets . . .

'I'm trying to keep it tidy,' I told him.

'Well, you should try harder,' he said, and smacked me hard across the face.

It was the first of many, many beatings. Sometimes he hit me because he said he could smell dirty nappies, or because I wasn't keeping the room tidy, or because Debbie cried out in the night. Sometimes he hit me because I was taking Debbie to the pool but other times he hit me because I wasn't taking her to the pool.

Sometimes he hit me for no reason at all.

Before I got to Cobar, I'd fondly and naively assumed Colin's parents would keep him in check and protect me. But night after night, as I screamed when he gave me another belting, no one came to help. At first, I thought his parents didn't care. Then, when I saw him hit his dad one day in the kitchen for getting in his way, I understood they were scared of him too.

I wondered if this was how all men behaved. I was only sixteen and had only my dad as a role model. He'd regularly beaten me black and blue, and now here was my husband doing the same. I assumed this was normal; this was how everyone lived. I'd just have to put up with it. This was the price I had to pay for keeping

Debbie and having a roof over our heads and food on the table.

I think, in retrospect, Colin was just born violent. It's how he expressed himself. It was how he communicated. When he was sober, he was quiet and withdrawn and surly. But as soon as he started drinking – and that was most days – he'd lash out at anything and everything. However careful you were around him, you were never right, things were never good enough.

It was worse at night. If he hadn't had too much to drink, he'd want sex and, as his wife, I had no right to deprive him. But I later learnt that Colin's version of sex wasn't like other people's. It was more like rape. He'd behave like an animal, clawing at me, hitting me and forcing himself into me. Often, I couldn't help crying out and sometimes I'd even scream in terror and pain. His parents had the bedroom next door and you can't tell me they didn't know what was going on. They couldn't have missed it. I'd turn up at the breakfast table the next morning with a black eye, or my face cut, or my lip swollen, with bruises all over my legs and arms, and they never said a word. I don't think I can ever forgive them for that.

One morning, after a particularly terrible battering, I went to feed Debbie and couldn't express any milk. I was almost dry. To me, this was the final straw. I could withstand anything to keep my daughter safe but if Colin's violence was now affecting her, I knew I'd have to do something. Back in those days, the police weren't interested in domestic violence. They stayed well away. Other people too weren't sympathetic; that wasn't their business and they didn't want to stick their noses in. I knew the only two people who could help me were back in Sydney: Keith and his mum.

I plotted my escape carefully and acted normally for the next few days. Happily, my milk started to come back too. Then, on a Wednesday morning when Colin and his dad had left for work and Mrs O'Brien had gone out to do some shopping, I packed up my measly possessions – everything except that shocking green dress – and walked out with Debbie in my arms to the train station.

I was running away yet again.

Chapter Thirteen
My Little Runaway

Back in Granville, Keith immediately dubbed me his 'little runaway' just like the song. He was thrilled to see me, his mum less so. Thankfully, they both loved meeting Debbie and said what a beautiful, sunny baby she was. But when I asked if I could stay for a few days while I got myself sorted, Mrs Morris refused.

'I'm sorry, Dianne,' she said. 'I truly am. But you can't sleep here under the same roof as Keith. If the police find out, they'll start asking questions again about whether he's really your baby's dad and then, well, you know how that could end up.'

I was devastated, but I tried hard not to show it.

'Mum,' Keith said, 'how about we look after Debbie at night, while Dianne goes to stay at a friend's? That'd be okay, wouldn't it?'

His mother looked doubtful.

'Oh come on, Mum, please. It's going to be hard for her to stay at a friend's with a baby in tow.'

'All right,' she eventually said.

'Thanks so much, Mrs Morris! That's great. And Debbie is so good. I'll express some milk into a bottle for her night feed.'

For the next month, Debbie stayed at their house, while we told Mrs Morris I was sleeping at a friend's. In truth, I was actually sleeping in their backyard in their empty dog's kennel. I couldn't bear to be apart from my daughter and I didn't have too many friends left in the area. I thought about going to see Shirley, but I preferred to stay close. So I'd say goodnight, and walk off around the corner, then double back, climb over their back fence, and settle down for the night in the kennel. I'd hear Keith – bless him – get up every night at about 2 a.m., warm Debbie's bottle and then go back to bed to feed her or come out to see me and we'd feed her together. I thought I'd never loved him more. We grew closer and closer and sometimes he'd visit me alone and we'd make quiet love together and fall asleep with our limbs all tangled. And, of course, he never hit me, or showed the slightest sign of wanting to.

Back then, it was hard for young, single mothers. There was no pension, no allowance. You could receive the child endowment payment, which was then about two pounds for a single child, but because I was still married, I wasn't eligible for any other help. I knew how hard it would be to find a job and care for my daughter at the same time. The alternative was going to the police station and pleading poverty to receive a voucher for milk and bread, or visiting the Salvation Army food kitchen. But Keith was adamant that he'd look after me.

A friend of his told him about some work available in Walgett, a wool, wheat and cotton town around 700 kilometres north-west of Sydney. I'd stopped there on our way to Cobar. I was reluctant at first; I wanted to stay in Sydney and start looking for my real parents, if they were still alive. The more time I spent away, I reasoned, the harder it would be to find them. But of course it was ridiculous living in a dog kennel, and I knew that couldn't last. Keith's friend had a car and said it would be so easy for us to drive out there. We could always come back if it didn't work out. Eventually, the three of us plus Debbie piled into the vehicle and headed back into the bush. Keith soon found a job in a sawmill just outside Walgett, and a kindly farmer said I could stay on the verandah of his shearing shed if I made sure to keep out of sight of the shearers.

Women weren't allowed inside the shed, so I made a little room on the wooden verandah for me and Debbie with planks of wood and blankets, and we hid there during the day while Keith was at work. It was lucky for me that she was such a good baby and barely cried. I'd sit there all day with her, trying to entertain her to keep her quiet. I'd make little toys out of wooden sticks – I'd learnt how from watching Uncle Walter carve his wooden toys in our backyard in Granville – and play and talk with her.

Occasionally, I'd take her out for a walk down to the Namoi River and sit on the banks and stare at the water. After the dry dustiness of Cobar, being by a river again felt simply delicious. It was soothing and often we'd be joined by a flock of magpies that didn't seem at all worried about a young mum and her baby. But I never stayed too long. I was always nervous we might be seen and reported to social welfare and then I'd run the risk of having Debbie taken off me. That was my constant fear.

I stuck it out on the shearing shed verandah for another month, but realised it was no way to look after a baby. We celebrated her first birthday in that room, and her first steps, but she needed a proper place to live, and I needed a kitchen to prepare her better meals and more than just a tap a walk away to wash her nappies. Keith wasn't earning enough money at the sawmill to pay rent on a house as well as buy food for us all. In my heart, I knew we couldn't continue this way for much longer.

One day, I was sitting in the park near the river with Debbie, feeding the magpies with some crusts of old bread, when an Aboriginal man approached us. I was used to seeing black people as nearly half the Walgett population was Aboriginal, but he was blacker than anyone I'd ever seen. Indeed, he was so black, he was almost purple. As he came closer, I could see he was wearing some kind of traditional dress, with a loin cloth, an animal skin cloak and body paint on his bare chest. He was also holding a spear.

'G'day,' he said.

'G'day,' I said back.

He then squatted down. 'Are you new in town? Good to see more blackfellas here.'

I was puzzled. 'We're just passing through, but we're not blackfellas. We're from Sydney.'

He looked amused. 'Right enough you're blackfellas. Do you

honestly not know that? I could tell as soon as I saw you, and your baby too.'

'No, I've always had darker skin,' I said. 'I don't know who my parents are, but I'm maybe Italian, or Irish, or had a black American dad ... or ...'

'Aboriginal,' he said, finishing my sentence for me. He laughed, showing a full set of dazzling white teeth. 'Well, good luck, let those magpies look out for you, and see you around.' With that, he stood up and loped off into the bush.

It was July 1963 and Walgett was fast becoming something of a national flashpoint for Aboriginal rights. Some of the local Indigenous people had been protesting against discrimination, about where they were allowed to live and the weird unofficial segregation that existed, and had taken to wearing traditional dress to make themselves more visible. Their anger was mounting. Two years later, a group of students from the University of Sydney, inspired by the 1961 Freedom Rides in the US, got on a bus and toured regional towns to tell national media about racist acts against Aboriginal people.

These 'Freedom Riders', led by a man called Charles Perkins who was later to become the pin-up for Aboriginal rights in Australia, stopped first in Walgett to demonstrate outside the local RSL club, which they'd heard wouldn't admit Indigenous ex-servicemen, and a clothes shop that didn't allow black women to try on dresses. As they left the town afterwards, some people tried to force their bus off the road. It made the news nationally, and internationally.

I wondered about what that Aboriginal man had said to me.

Was I Aboriginal? I shook my head. I had to find my real parents, and soon, to find out what, and who, I was. It would also be wonderful for Debbie to be able to meet the rest of her family.

*

I turned seventeen the following day and marked the occasion with a special breakfast of bread and jam. But as soon as I started eating, I felt sick. I got up and ran off to throw up. I had a sudden thought and checked my dates. With a sinking feeling, I realised I'd missed my last period. Could life really get any harder? I fell to my knees and prayed to God to give me a break. Surely I deserved one by now.

I spent the whole day mulling over my options. I loved Keith and was happy, in one way, that I was having his baby, but on the other hand I knew he couldn't support me and Debbie, let alone a second child. I stood even less chance of finding a job as a pregnant single mum. But I couldn't stay living here on a shearing shed verandah. It was no place for kids, or for me.

That evening, when Keith came back, the only thing I told him about my day was that strange encounter with the Aboriginal man. He was interested, but I could see he was exhausted from work. I let him fall asleep without even mentioning my suspicions that he might soon become a father.

The next day, I paid a visit to the local doctor. He did a test and confirmed what I'd thought: I was two months pregnant and my baby was due in January. I walked around the whole of Walgett with Debbie in my arms, trying to work out what to do. I looked in the window of a real estate agency and saw how much rents were – they were totally beyond us. I looked at noticeboards for any jobs – but there was nothing I'd be able to do with a baby. It felt, yet again, that my options were narrowing.

Late in the afternoon, I phoned Colin's sister Sue. She said that Colin and his parents were really upset that I'd left and were worried about me.

'But they were so nasty to me,' I said, tears pouring down my face. 'I don't think they cared about us at all.'

'Oh, they do. They realise now how much they miss you. Please come back. I'll send you some money for the train fare. Where are you?' I hesitated. She sensed my wariness. 'No, Dianne, honestly, we'd all love you to come back. Colin's very sorry for how he treated you. And we all miss Debbie, of course. How is she doing?'

'She's fine,' I said. 'She's okay. Actually, Sue ... I've just discovered I'm pregnant again.'

To my surprise, she sounded delighted. 'That's fantastic news! Colin will be so pleased.'

It hadn't occurred to her that I might be pregnant to someone else. I decided not to say anything that might make it harder for me. 'Well, you could send the money to the Walgett Post Office,' I said. 'I could pick it up there. Thanks a lot.'

'Great, I'll do that first thing tomorrow,' Sue said. 'And Dianne ...'

'Yes?'

'Please come home soon.'

I didn't know what to do. Keith was my soulmate and after so much time apart and so many hurdles, we were finally together. But I now had the wellbeing of two children to think about, and their futures. This was going to be the hardest decision of my life.

A week later, when Keith came home from the sawmill, we went out to buy some food and came back to the room and ate it by candlelight. Afterwards, we made love with an intensity that brought tears to my eyes.

The next morning, when he'd left for work, I took Debbie to the station.

Chapter Fourteen
Happy Families

I was greeted in Cobar like a returning hero. Colin met me at the station and hugged me, then took Debbie and carried her carefully to the car. Mrs O'Brien kissed me on the cheek and said I could do the washing any day I wanted. Even Mr O'Brien patted me on the shoulder and said he was glad to see me. Colin's sister Sue beamed and I half wondered if she'd told them to show up and be on their best behaviour.

I hoped that appearances weren't deceiving and this time we could really be a happy family. And at first, we were. Colin was much more attentive to Debbie and played with her and cooed at her like any doting dad. He was nice to me and didn't shout or lash out. He told me he'd applied for a Housing Commission house and that he was looking forward to us having another baby. I felt a bit guilty about that but then reminded myself he'd be a better father if he thought the child was his. Even Mrs O'Brien was considerate and, true to her word, I did my washing any day I pleased.

The day we were told by the government's housing department that we'd been allocated a two-bedroom place of our own, I was over the moon. It was September 1963 and I was around four months pregnant. I wanted to make sure I created a lovely home for Debbie and the new baby. We moved in and, even better, Colin started to get more mining work out in the bush, so he was often away for days at a time. Life was suddenly peaceful, and I allowed myself to dream that it might stay this way.

Of course it didn't last. Colin started drinking again. Sometimes he was so out of it, I don't think he quite knew what he was doing. Maybe I was just the handiest person, or thing, for him to let his anger out on. His eyes would roll, he would roar and I'd know, as I could feel the hair prickle on the back of my neck, that I was in for it. At first, I tried to defend myself and fight back the way the Harrisons had taught me. But while I could catch him by surprise on occasion, most of the time he'd just fight harder and heavier and nastier. Very soon I learnt it was better to just stand there and take it, and do my crying and patching up later.

Whenever he came home smelling of rum, I made sure to get Debbie safely out of harm's way. Naturally, I wanted to protect her from the sight and sounds of the violence. I'd bite my lip so I wouldn't scream or cry out. Other times, when I knew he was on his way home, especially with a pay cheque that he'd stop off at the pub to cash, I'd give Debbie her tea early, close the curtains of her room, and put her to bed in the hope she might fall asleep and be oblivious to her father's behaviour.

It was hard, it was exhausting and it was horribly worrying, especially with another baby on the way. I lived in fear I might lose it, but the bigger fear was leaving Colin and then losing my baby and Debbie to social welfare because I couldn't support them.

I stuck it out with Colin that second time for a couple of months, but then phoned my Uncle Ken. Mum had once said he'd take care of me if something happened. I'd found out he lived in Bateau Bay on the NSW Central Coast, which was near our old holiday spot Budgewoi, and I asked Sue if she'd lend me the train and bus fare. She handed it over without hesitation. She knew what was happening with Colin and I think she felt bad she'd persuaded me to come back to Cobar.

Uncle Ken and Aunty Peg were delighted to see me again after all this time and said that they'd contacted my dad to find out where I was and how I'd been going, but he'd hung up on them. They were thrilled to see I had such a gorgeous little daughter, and another child on the way.

'I'm so glad you've made your way here, Dianne, dear,' Aunty Peg said. 'It really is so wonderful to see you. We've been so worried.'

It was lovely to be back with family, and with someone who reminded me so much of Mum and whom I could talk to and remember the past with.

'She was a beaut mum all right,' Uncle Ken said, his eyes misty. 'She always thought the world of you and Ronnie. You two kept her going throughout all the ...' He stopped, suddenly.

'All the what?' I asked.

'Well, the difficulties of your dad,' he said guardedly.

'What do you mean?' I asked.

He sighed. 'Your mum and dad were happy at first. I never warmed to your dad, but Val seemed to love him, so we tried to as well. But then, I don't know, they started to argue, and she was obviously very unhappy.'

'And then what?' I asked, intrigued.

'She started getting sick a lot,' Uncle Ken said. 'She didn't know what it was and neither did we. She went to that doctor your dad put her onto, but he didn't seem to do much for her.'

'Yes, I remember,' I said. 'She started staying in bed a lot.'

'That's right,' Uncle Ken said. 'But no one could put their finger on exactly what was wrong with her.'

'It was a weak, worn-out heart,' I said. 'That's what the doctor told me.'

'Yes,' said Uncle Ken, sounding doubtful. 'Yes, that must have been what it was. Now, are you going to stay with us? What are your plans?'

And Mum somehow got lost in the rest of the conversation.

*

It was easy staying with Uncle Ken and Aunty Peg. They lived close to the Tuggerah Lake, which I loved, and they were happy to mind Debbie during the day, which meant, at last, I could go back to work and start earning some money. There was a limit to what I could do, being five months pregnant, but I managed to find a job in a jeans factory. It was boring work, but I loved the feeling of being a little more independent again.

In the middle of my shift one day, after two weeks working there, however, I had a strange feeling that something was wrong with Debbie. I phoned Uncle Ken's house, but there was no answer. I phoned an hour later, and still nothing. My uneasiness was growing. I asked my boss if I could leave early and come in early the next day to make up for it. He agreed and I raced for the bus to get back.

When I arrived, Uncle Ken and Aunty Peg were ashen-faced. Colin had been round, they said, and had been waving a birth certificate saying it proved Debbie was his and if they didn't hand her over, he'd do something terrible. They'd felt they had little choice.

'But how did he know I was here?' I asked through my tears.

My uncle and aunt exchanged meaningful looks. 'We think your dad must have told him where we live,' Uncle Ken said. 'Remember, he was always very tight with Colin.'

I remembered that only too well. As time passed, I'd suspected he set me up with Colin in a bid to get rid of me. Now he was trying to destroy me again. I caught the first train to Sydney and went to the office of the Federal Police. They quickly assessed the situation, looked at Debbie's birth certificate that I'd kept in my maiden name – thank God! – said I could charge Colin with kidnapping my daughter, and offered to drive me back to Cobar. That was the last place on earth I wanted to go, but I'd do anything to get Debbie back. We drove for ten hours through the night and arrived at our house early the next morning.

Mr and Mrs O'Brien were there with Debbie. We barged in and I snatched her up off her grandmother's lap. I think she was too shocked to resist.

'Where's Colin?' I demanded.

'He's in the bush,' his mum replied.

'So how did he find me?'

'Your dad heard through someone else in your family that you'd turned up on the coast,' she said. 'So Colin went straight over there as soon as he heard. He missed Debbie so much. We all did. He did the first thing that came into his head and took her. When he realised later what he'd done, honestly, Dianne, he was genuinely sorry ...'

The police asked me if I wanted to press charges. I was in two minds. It touched me that Colin had missed Debbie and, seeing his mum there, her shoulders hunched, looking so broken and sad, made me feel a rush of sympathy for the family. Mrs O'Brien seemed a lot softer than I remembered.

'She's so young to have a baby,' I heard her telling the police. 'I didn't think she'd care not to have her. I thought she'd be happy to get on with her life.'

I shook my head. These people were so screwed up themselves, they thought I'd be the same. And I most definitely wasn't.

Finally, the officers took me aside. 'What would you like to do?' they asked me. 'We can arrest your husband for kidnapping if you want. It's up to you. But if he's away in the bush, and you don't have anywhere else to go ...'

I looked at Debbie. She'd scrambled out of my arms, had been darting around the room between all the adults and was now looking up at Mrs O'Brien, holding out her arms to be picked up. 'Nanna!' she said. 'Nanna!' She didn't seem at all harmed by her experience. Mrs O'Brien looked at me, and I nodded my permission, then she swung her up high into the air and she giggled delightedly.

I sighed. This was her home, the only home she'd ever really known, and, like it or lump it, this was her family. With only a few months to go before I'd have a brother or sister for her, was it really fair to drag her away back around the country again?

'It's okay, officer,' I said finally. 'I won't press charges, and I'll stay here. But thank you so much for all your help.'

'That's all right, Mrs O'Brien,' the one in charge said. 'Any time. Glad it could all be sorted out.'

*

My problem was that I always felt for the underdog, the person who'd messed up with the sad face, the one begging for a second chance. I was such an innocent in the ways of the world. When someone told me they had my best interests at heart, I believed them. When they said they'd made a terrible mistake and would do better next time, I took that at face value. And when they said they were sorry, that they were ashamed of whatever it was they'd done and swore they'd never do it again, I fell for it, hook, line and sinker. I wanted to believe the best in people no matter how many times I was disappointed.

In some, such an optimistic outlook might be considered a charming trait. In me, it made me an easy target. Colin, for instance, was never going to change, but I clung on to the hope that I'd somehow be able to bring out the best in him. Even though he started hitting me again after only a few days, I kept on thinking – and hoping – he might change. As Debbie grew even more gorgeous and as the birth of what Colin thought was his second child grew closer, I assumed he'd soften. That was a hard-won lesson.

He was just a cruel, cruel bastard. There was something in him that was warped. He was the absolute opposite of me. As a kid, I'd adored my dog Lassie, so thought I'd get Debbie a dog. He was a small bitsa – a bit of this, a bit of that – a real cutie of a stray I picked up off death row at the dog pound. Debbie loved him, and he bounded around after her everywhere she went. Six weeks after I brought her home, she was dead. Colin had run over her in his wagon. He swore it was an accident, but I never believed him.

I always had a little menagerie of animals around me: cats, birds, even a pet piglet called Piggy I reared by hand and kept in a sawn-off water tank in the backyard. I once even adopted a little joey that wandered into the yard, who'd obviously lost his mother. That baby kangaroo followed me all around the house, the garden and sometimes, when he jumped over the back fence, all the way to the shops. We became a common sight around Cobar, me and Rooey, with Piggy following hot on our heels. Debbie loved them too. Then a keeper turned up from Dubbo Zoo saying he'd received a phone call that I was illegally keeping a kangaroo.

'I don't know what you're talking about,' I told him. 'I don't have a kangaroo here.'

He raised an eyebrow. 'Really? So what's that brown thing behind you?'

I turned round. Rooey had jumped over the gate I'd put up in the kitchen to keep him there, and had come to say hello.

'Oh no, please don't take him,' I pleaded. 'He's so tame and we're caring for him.'

The keeper didn't care. And Rooey was taken, too. No guesses who'd phoned the zoo.

I'd often sit on the verandah, listening to the radio and looking longingly east in the direction of Sydney. My old guitar teacher Jimmy Little was on the radio regularly now with his number one hit 'Royal Telephone' about having a direct line to Jesus. I'd listen to his beautiful smooth voice singing the gospel song, and then pray to God, asking Him why He was putting me through all this. If only it was as easy as Jimmy sang it was, I thought to myself. If only I'd had a dad like Jimmy. Life would have been so, so different.

Jimmy came to Cobar once to play in a concert and I managed to say hello to him before he went on stage. He seemed pleased to see me and, halfway through his set, he stopped and talked about his life. 'You know,' he said, 'there's a young girl here in the audience I taught to play guitar.' He looked straight at me and my heart stopped, fearing that, just like Mum had done when I was a kid, he'd haul me up to demonstrate. Thankfully, he didn't. I had Debbie on my lap and I was pregnant but, more importantly, I really couldn't play very well.

On a hot summer's night a couple of months before I was due to give birth, Colin came home late from the pub, woke me up and told me to get dressed. We were going up to the Great Western Hotel to meet a few of his friends. I was plainly showing and feeling terrible, so I told him I'd be better off staying in bed. But he insisted. I got dressed and half-walked, and was half-dragged, to the bar. When we arrived, one of his mates said I seemed really sick and Colin should take me home. At that, Colin looked me up and down and then exploded. He grabbed me and dragged me out onto the street. 'I'll teach you for embarrassing me in front of my friends! You're not making a fool of me!' He then started hitting me.

I curled up into a ball to protect my baby from the rain of blows and kicks when I heard a car screech to a halt and a door open and slam shut. A deep man's voice ordered Colin to get away from me. Colin stopped immediately.

'That's right,' the man said. 'And if I ever see you hit her again, you're dead. You hear me? *You're dead.*'

I was so grateful someone had intervened on my behalf but then I also half-wished Colin would hit me again as I lay there, just in case this man was as good as his word.

Chapter Fifteen
Better the Devil You Know

I was at my lowest ebb and I think I started giving off the air of a hapless victim. I was only seventeen and had no one in my corner to protect me or help me or advise me on how to get out of this terrible mess. I was completely lost. It never occurred to me that people would take advantage of someone when they're at their most vulnerable, and then kick them when they're down.

After the street bashing, I fled Cobar once again, terrified I'd lose the baby to Colin's fists and feet. I went back to Granville, after making sure Sue would feed my cats and Piggy in my absence. It was the only place where I knew I had some friends. Keith was in Queensland and seeing another woman, so I couldn't go to his mum's, so I thought I'd try an old schoolfriend, Melanie. I went to her house and her brother Hugh opened the door, someone I'd also known from our dancing days. He hugged me and said his sister was out, but I should come in and wait for her, and have a look at the new TV their mum had just bought them.

I lifted the buggy with Debbie inside over the front step and parked her in the sitting room, then sank into the sofa next to her. I was now huge, and my legs hurt and my feet were throbbing. Hugh was in the kitchen and we idly chatted while he boiled the kettle. We caught up on all our news and I told him things weren't working out too well for me.

'Oh right?' he said, coming into the lounge room and sitting down beside me, very close. Too close.

It didn't feel comfortable, but I thought he'd maybe just misjudged the space. 'No, it's not too good over in Cobar,' I said uneasily.

He put his arm round me, but it wasn't a comforting, brotherly gesture. It felt more like a come on. Then his hand went down to one of my breasts.

'No, Hugh,' I said. 'What are you doing? Stop that.'

He didn't, and me resisting just seemed to excite him more.

'Hugh! I'm seven months pregnant! Get off me. Please!'

'Come on, Dianne,' he wheedled. 'You know you want me.'

'No!' I said. 'Look! My daughter's just there. Stop!'

But he didn't. He just carried on fondling my breasts and tried to push me onto my back.

'No!' I said again, standing up with great difficulty because of my size, the softness of the sofa and Hugh's weight. 'No. Stop. I didn't come here for ...'

He pushed me back down with such force, I couldn't stay upright.

This is the oldest photo that exists of me, at eight months of age, sitting on an old wicker chair on the verandah of our house at the wheat farm in Parkes, central west NSW.

Aged about two, I'm pictured with my beloved mum, after picking what looks suspiciously like a handful of weeds for her at the park. I probably thought they were flowers.

After Mum, Dad was the centre of my world and I thought he always would be. It was only later that I realised something was terribly wrong. We're pictured here together in front of the farmhouse at Parkes.

Dad must have seemed to everyone else like the perfect father, and here he was, playing Father Christmas for me when I was about eight years old. But after the incident in the bedroom the year before, I was always cautious and uneasy around him. I think you can see that in my face.

My 'gang' of misfits at school. I always befriended anyone who got picked on, or was smaller or more timid than the others. As you can see, even at twelve years old, I was much taller and bigger than the other girls.

I loved my guitar lessons with our neighbour, musician Jimmy Little. I was never terribly good, but I just adored hanging out with him. At thirteen, I already looked a lot older than my age.

My world came to a shuddering halt after Mum died suddenly in April 1961, when I was fourteen. I was devastated and wore black to show how much I loved and missed her. Dad took this photo of me in front of his FJ Holden.

The loves of my life – my children. Left to right: David, Debbie, Kevin at the top, Cindy below centre, Linda and Phillip.

The opening of an elders' hostel in Shepparton in 1995, when I was forty-nine, with my great-uncle Emmanuel Cooper and a photo of Aboriginal activist William Cooper, who was Emmanuel's second cousin and my great-grandfather.

At the hospital in Gosford on the NSW Central Coast, where I was working in health.

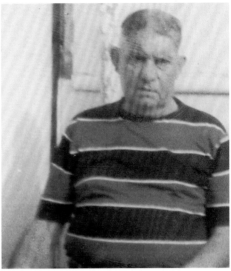

My birth mother, Esme. I'd spent so many years searching for her, but perhaps, by the time I'd found her, we'd been apart too long. We never had that mother–daughter tie I'd so fondly hoped for.

My birth father, Steve Hamilton. Sadly, my birth mother never introduced me to him while he was alive and only told me his name after he'd died, robbing me of the chance to meet him and get to know him.

It was always lovely to bump into my cousin Jimmy Little around the traps, and we laughed to think we'd been related all those years ago, but had never known it. We're pictured here in 2004 with my cousin 'Birdie'.

Here I am, at age seventy-four, at Mingaletta, an Aboriginal and Torres Strait Islander community hub on the NSW Central Coast. I'm proud of the services we provide to improve the quality of life for both our people and anyone else who needs help.

Then he ripped at my clothes, clawed at my stockings and attacked me like an animal on heat. There was nothing I could do. I was so shocked, so stunned. I'd grown up with Hugh and Melanie. He was the last person I'd ever imagined would do something like this.

By the time I managed to stumble out of the house, sobbing, my clothes torn, I'd completely lost faith in mankind. If an old childhood friend could do something like that to me, what hope could I have for any kind of future? I caught the next train back to Cobar.

Better the devil you know.

*

When I got home, I tried to work out a survival strategy. Sydney no longer offered an escape so I'd have to make a go of it out west. I found the stifling heat of the summers oppressive, the winds that blew the dust into every nook and cranny of the house tiresome, and the willy-willies – the mini-tornadoes that often tore through – scary. On the other hand, there was the swimming pool, and with Debbie much more confident and being able to doggy-paddle, I could go there more often and just relax in the water.

More importantly, I decided to make the effort to make some friends, and looked deliberately for people beyond Colin and his family's influence. They seemed to know nearly everyone in town, and most people were scared of Colin. I found my new friends in an area to the south of Cobar called Cornish Town, where there was no running water or electricity, and houses were made out of corrugated iron and flattened kerosene tins and rough pieces of wood and whatever else anyone could get their hands on. This was where the poorest people lived. In the old days, miners lived there, but now it'd been taken over by the 'displaced persons' who had migrated to Australia after World War II, mostly from Eastern Europe, and the local Aboriginals.

It was a ramshackle kind of place, but I found the people there welcoming, non-judgemental and happy to take me at face value. They didn't seem hell-bent on taking advantage of me, either. They knew what it was like to be downtrodden and powerless. They weren't well off, had the worst jobs and lived in the scruffiest part of town. They were often discriminated against and treated as second-class citizens. We had a bit in common.

But it was those people who helped me slowly recover my self-confidence and build my determination to start mounting my fightback. There was one woman I became particularly friendly with, a black woman called Dolly. She had a big family, and I'd often take Debbie and wander down there during the day to sit and drink tea with her, while Debbie played with her kids. I talked to her a lot about Colin and how he treated me, and she would listen and be sympathetic. Sometimes, when Colin was away, I'd babysit for Dolly. It was great to have a woman friend. I still had Colin's sister Sue, but I felt if she had to choose between me and her brother, she'd probably choose him. Dolly and her family, on the other hand, adopted me as one of their own.

Whenever Colin found out I'd been to Cornish Town to see my mates, he bashed me as he said I shouldn't be going down there and mixing with people like them.

'Oh, I should stay here with people like *you*, should I?' I said to him once. 'People who hit me and don't want me to have any freedom?'

'No, it's just because I care,' he said.

'Funny way of showing it,' I mumbled, then got a punch in the chest for my cheek.

It was strange: Colin didn't want me going anywhere without him, yet I knew for a fact that he'd started sleeping with other women around town. I'd had my suspicions, then my new friends confirmed they'd seen him with a couple of other women at various pubs, slobbering over them with his hand up their dresses. But my mates helped me get even. They showed me how to put food on his account at the local shop, which was taken directly out of his wages before he got them. I also started practising driving in his car. I'd never had any lessons, but drove round and round the local streets until I felt I knew what I was doing.

One afternoon, I crushed a Serepax someone had given me for anxiety and put it in his sandwich in the hope that, mixed with alcohol, he might go to sleep early and not bash me. It worked a treat, but I was so nervous he might not wake up, I had to constantly check his breathing, and vowed never to do it again. And I'd always wanted a washing machine, which Colin refused to buy. This time, I bought one from a local store that offered credit, in his name.

I passed him standing in the main street drinking when the delivery guy drove down the road. 'There goes your washing machine!' he cackled nastily. He hadn't realised the man was heading to our house. I loved doing the washing in that machine, and often Dolly came over and did her washing in it too.

When he found out about the money, the car and the washing machine, he went mad. I stood my ground and said I wanted a divorce.

He glared at me. 'I'll kill you first!'

'You wouldn't dare,' I replied, although I thought he probably would.

*

In January 1964, his mum, Mrs O'Brien, was taken suddenly ill and died a few days later. Colin was beside himself and swore, on her deathbed, he'd never drink again. A few days later, he turned up dead drunk to her funeral. He was out of control.

I gave birth on 22 January 1964 to another girl, whom I called Linda. Colin came to the hospital to see us and said he had something for me. From his pocket, he produced a paper bag.

'What's inside?' I asked.

'Ham sandwiches,' he said.

I looked at him, stunned. 'No. No, you wouldn't.'

'Yes I would,' he replied with a triumphant look. 'You couldn't come to Piggy, so I brought Piggy to you.'

*

We continued in this awful way, but at least I had my two daughters, a roof over our heads, a car I could drive – even though I didn't have a licence – and a new way of extracting money from my husband.

He was away more and more with his work for the mine, with rumours some of the other mines were likely to reopen soon thanks to new methods of mining and the rising price of copper.

Whenever Colin was on night shift and at home during the day, I'd take the kids down to the pool, or visit friends in Cornish Town and help them out with their babies. I celebrated my eighteenth birthday at Dolly's house, surrounded by the warm glow of my new friendships. I'd only take the girls home when I was sure Colin would be out. The sole person who ever came to see me when he was around was Sue. Everyone else stayed away. If I happened to be there when he came home, just as I used to do with Debbie, I'd close the curtains and put both girls to bed early in the hope they'd sleep through the bashing and raping. It was the only way I knew how to cope.

When Linda was about ten months old, Colin gave me a particularly severe battering. The next day, I was trying to clear up the mess he'd made, when I felt a sharp pain in my stomach. I doubled over and was able to crawl to the phone to call an ambulance. In the hospital, they told me I'd lost a baby boy. I'd been three and a half months pregnant.

I was devastated, but there was a silver lining. Maybe Colin realised he'd gone too far, or maybe it was all too hard having to support a wife and two children, but he decided he wanted to be free again and I wasn't going to stop him. The afternoon he was due to pick up a tax refund cheque, he collected it from the tax office and then vanished, presumably to Sydney.

I didn't care. I got a job cleaning in the pubs in town, and Dolly babysat for me while I worked. I babysat for her in return, and then for other people around town, and took in ironing, just like my mum had done. It was late 1964 and the girls and I had a house, we had friends and, at last, we had a future.

Chapter Sixteen
The Kindness of Strangers

Life suddenly felt different. I'd never been afraid of hard work and I enjoyed going out and earning money, knowing the girls were being looked after. I still didn't like Cobar, but it would do for a while. I had time to start thinking about how I might trace my real parents. I was anxious to know who I was, and for my kids to know who their family might be. But the longer I left it, the harder it would be. It would be horrendous to track down my parents, only to discover they might recently have passed away.

Now that I'd turned eighteen, I thought I'd have more rights legally, and I called what was back then the NSW Child Welfare Department. I explained that I'd been adopted, that my adoptive mother had since died, and that I wanted to made contact with my birth mother and father. They were extraordinarily unhelpful and suggested I talk to my adoptive dad. I tried to explain that he wouldn't do anything for me, but they were adamant they couldn't give me any names. I tried writing to them, and then calling again, hoping I'd come across someone more sympathetic, but no joy. I hit a brick wall every time.

Someone then suggested I try a private detective. I asked around and eventually I was given the name of someone in Sydney. I called them, and they agreed to take on the job. I felt excited. This could be the break I'd been waiting for.

In the meantime, I led a relatively quiet life with the kids who seemed to be thriving without Colin around. I watched TV and followed the news about the Aboriginal Freedom Riders over in Walgett. An ABC TV journalist was reporting from the front door of the RSL club, which I recognised immediately. He said it had entertained a whole host of Aboriginal troops when they came back from fighting for their country in World War II. But the very next day, most of them were banned and weren't allowed in any of the other hotels in town, either. Instead, they were sold beer through the back windows at three times the price. I was appalled to think people could be treated that way. As the Aboriginal protesters moved on to other towns, I followed their progress keenly.

I tried to get out and about every once in a while and made a few more friends. Just after my nineteenth birthday in July 1965, I started going out with a quiet man I met after I saw him chopping wood at the back of the police station. Michael Brown had just split up with his girlfriend and was both good looking and good company. Two months later, however, I missed my period and discovered I was pregnant again. Three months after that, Michael went back to his old girlfriend. I was heartbroken.

I decided I needed a change of scene, so I took the girls back to Sydney. When we arrived, I went to the Salvation Army and asked if they had somewhere we could stay. They sent us to the La Perouse Women's and Children's Home, set up for wives who'd left violent marriages and didn't have the funds to rent, or buy, a place of their own. It was in the Old Cable Station by the sea in the eastern suburbs, and was later turned into the local museum.

I received some money from the government now to help with living expenses for the kids. There was a payment for each child – child endowment – and, that year, the government also introduced a social welfare payment known as 'mother's allowance' for single women with children. It wasn't much, but it was better than nothing.

I liked the La Perouse area as it had long had an Aboriginal community living there. Like Dolly and her mates, they were warm and welcoming. But the girls kept being bitten by sandflies, sometimes so badly they'd end up in hospital, and the stern red-brick building reminded me a little too much of the other institutions I'd been in after Mum had died. I wondered if Dad might now have softened enough to help me out, and I naively thought he might like to meet his granddaughters. Surely, seeing how beautiful they were would melt his heart? I'd also heard he'd split up from his last girlfriend and was now living with a new woman.

When I walked up Redfern Street in Granville, I indeed saw a different woman standing in the front garden of our house, watering the plants. As I came closer I noticed she was moving very slowly and looked very pale. I stopped at the front gate, called her over and introduced myself.

She said she knew who I was, and cooed over the children, but said Dad wasn't there. Then she started looking anxiously up the street. 'I'm sorry, but I think you'd better be going now,' she said. 'I honestly don't think he'll want to see you.'

'But the girls ...' I said pleadingly.

She wrung her hands. 'No, no, you should leave now before he finds out I've been talking to you.'

I realised at that moment two things: one, that nothing had changed; and two, that she was scared of him. I insisted on leaving my phone number with her – just in case – but when I said goodbye and walked away with the girls, she looked positively relieved.

That evening, I received a phone call from someone who said she was the daughter of Dad's new girlfriend.

'I'm so sorry to bother you,' she said, 'but Mum said you visited her today.'

'Yes, I did,' I said. 'What's the problem?'

'Well, I know this sounds weird, but I think there *is* a problem. Mum's been with your dad for a couple of years now and she's not really been herself since.'

My ears pricked up. 'What do you mean?'

'It's just that she ... she was always so healthy and fit and now she's just a shadow of her former self. We're really worried about her. She spends a lot of time in bed during the day and she never did that before. It's kind of like ... she's being poisoned or something.'

I felt suddenly sick. 'And this has only been since she's been with my dad?'

'Yes,' she said. 'I hope you don't mind me asking, but what did your mum die of?'

'I was told she had a weak heart,' I said. I thought for a moment. 'But of course I never knew that for sure. I was just a kid.'

'Thanks so much for telling me that,' she said. 'I think I need a good talk with Mum.'

'Good luck,' I said. And I truly meant it. At that moment, I decided I'd never visit Dad ever again. I couldn't prove anything, but I couldn't help wondering if he'd had something to do with Mum's ill health. He certainly had the motive – that money she'd saved for my inheritance – which could also explain his eagerness after her death to get me out of his life.

That night the dreaded shark nightmare was back.

*

A few days later, I bumped into an old schoolfriend who said she might be able to get me a caravan in Cabramatta to live in instead of the refuge. I jumped at the chance. Some people could be so kind. She was happy to help and I was able to get some welfare money from the Child Welfare Department. Social workers at the Crown Street Women's Hospital, where I'd had Debbie, were also ready to supplement our meagre income so we'd have enough to eat. And then, that Christmas, a Chinese man who had the caravan next door, and whose wife had just left him, invited me and the girls to visit the Blue Mountains with him and have a slap-up Christmas lunch at a local restaurant. I think he just wanted the company and to feel the warm glow of giving other people a good Christmas.

A few nights later, there was a knock on the caravan door. I opened it to find Michael Brown standing there.

'What are you doing here?' I gasped in surprise.

'I changed my mind,' he said. 'I missed you.'

'But what about your girlfriend?'

'I've told her I'm not coming back. I've come to collect you and the girls and my unborn baby and take you all up to northern NSW where my dad and his girlfriend have got a place. I thought we could make a go of it together there.'

I must have looked uncertain.

'C'mon, Di. Look at this place. Bringing up kids in a caravan ... We can do better than this. Come with me. It'll be good, you'll see.'

I weighed up the situation. The girls and I had been doing all right on our own. But Michael was right – the caravan wasn't ideal, especially when I'd have a new baby in there, too. Maybe he'd be a good dad to the baby when it was born, as well as to the girls. And I had to admit I still had a soft spot for him.

'Okay,' I said finally. 'Let's do it.'

He grinned and folded me into his arms.

It was the worst decision I ever made.

*

Michael's dad Alfred and his girlfriend Miriam – who was just four years older than Michael – lived in Iluka, a small fishing village nearly 700 kilometres north of Sydney. I was pleased that it was on the Clarence River, but that was about the only upside. The house smelled of pee; it hit you as soon as you walked through the front door. I soon found out why. Alfred had been crippled in a road accident in 1959 and now spent most of his time in bed. He'd pee in a pot that Miriam would then empty out of the window. The rest of the time, he'd get in his wheelchair and go fishing with Michael and it would usually end in a huge row. On one occasion, it was so bad, Michael left him in his chair, bogged in the sand, unable to move. I had to go down and rescue him.

I soon began to think there was something seriously wrong with Michael. Sometimes, he'd be sweet and caring, but at other times, he'd be angry and impatient and give me a backhander, or punch or kick me. Even worse, unlike Colin, he didn't seem to need a drink to turn violent, so you just never knew when it was coming. It made me watchful and anxious around him. One day, he told me to pack up the house as he and his dad had found work somewhere else and we were all moving. He went off with Alfred and Miriam, but said he'd be back that evening to pick us up. I spent the day packing and told the landlord we were off, then waited and waited for him to return to collect me and the girls.

He never did. He simply vanished.

The landlord, happily, took pity on us, and said I could take over the rent for ten bob a week. I did, and a couple of friends from Sydney came to stay for their holidays. It was lucky they were there. I started having labour pains when I was in the bath and couldn't get out on my own. They helped me out, then piled me into their little Morris car, which immediately got stuck in the sand. We were finally rescued by an ambulance that had to race to the river before the final ferry of the evening left for the other side, where the Maclean District Hospital was. By the time I got there, I was already exhausted.

My first baby boy was born on 7 April 1966 and I named him Kevin. The doctor told me he'd been a twin, but his brother hadn't developed in the womb. He was gorgeous in spite of having six fingers on one hand. The doctor said it was a common birth defect and that a lot of parents decided to have the extra finger removed.

'Yes, please take it off,' I said. 'I don't want the girls to see him like that. They'll be frightened.'

As a result, they never did, and they absolutely doted on him.

*

Life in Iluka was tough. I had that small social welfare payment for being a single mum which just about covered the rent and the child endowment, but it was still a struggle to make ends meet. With decimal currency coming in that year, the endowment had just gone up to $1.50 a week for a third child, which was handy, as well as the 50 cents I was getting for Debbie and the $1 for Linda as the second child. But $3 a week didn't stretch too far. Back then, a pint of milk cost 11 cents, a dozen eggs 65 cents and a couple of pounds of the cheapest chuck stewing steak a dollar.

To help us survive, I started baking fruit cakes to sell to the local shop and to anyone else who wanted to buy them. I'd push Kevin in his pram 8 kilometres out to the beach where I'd fish for food, and the girls would 'help' – after a fashion. If we were lucky, I'd gut and clean the fish there on the sand, build a fire to cook them and then we'd sit and eat. If we didn't catch anything, we'd go back home hungry, ready for some fruit cake to fill our bellies. Often, we'd find food left on the doorstep by generous neighbours who knew we were doing it tough. Looking back, I wonder how we coped. But we did. That said, I've never much liked fish or fruit cake since.

All the while, I made sure to let the private detective know where we were, just in case he managed to track down my real parents. It'd be wonderful, I thought, if I could make contact now. I felt sure they'd love to meet their grandchildren, and hoped they might be overjoyed to see me again, too. I'd never been more in need of a helping hand.

Five months later, Michael showed up again. He'd made another terrible mistake, he said, and really regretted leaving us. He'd come back to meet his son and see his step-daughters, and the woman he knew he loved. He was so charming, I fell for it again. I so desperately wanted to be part of a 'normal' family and knew we couldn't carry on much longer relying on the kindness of strangers.

*

We took off north, this time to Southport on Queensland's Gold Coast, about 200 kilometres north of Iluka. We moved into a caravan, ironically, given Michael's disapproval of my caravan in Cabramatta, and he found work in the local wreckers' yard. At first, things were okay. I was kept busy with the kids and would take them on long walks to what was my new favourite place, the banks of the Nerang River, or to the beach to play in the sand. But soon Michael was hitting me again and, in a caravan, you can't hide things like that from your kids – or your neighbours. They heard every blow, every whimper, every cry.

I told Michael we were leaving him but, again, he was remorseful.

'I'll make it better for you, Di, I promise,' he pleaded. 'I've got the chance of a flat at Surfers Paradise. It's really nice there and it'll be so much better than being cramped in this caravan.'

I could feel myself weakening and I knew he knew it.

'We could be happy there,' he said. 'Really happy. Debbie, Linda, Kevin ... and us. We'll be a real family.'

God help me, but I swallowed it again. We decamped to Surfers, a half-hour's drive south, and moved into the two-floor flat. Soon after, Michael's dad Alfred and Miriam moved in too. That hadn't been part of the deal, but Michael wouldn't hear a word against them. I loathed them. They were dirty, stank the place out and once I caught them having sex in the kitchen. It was no place for a mother and her three children. But when I complained to Michael, the violence started afresh. By this time, I was pregnant again, but he didn't seem to care.

'If I want, I'll just kick this baby out of you,' he threatened me. 'Is that what you want?'

I shut up then. There was nothing more precious to me than my kids and if I had to put up with bashings to keep them safe, then I would. Again, I was trapped, but even more tightly this time, with three children and another on the way, and the unending cycle of violence. There were the mood swings, the accusations, the recriminations, and then the beatings. I'd try to make sure the kids were either out, or in bed, when Michael came home from the wreckers' yard. One time, he got back early, told the kids to face the wall so they wouldn't witness the beating, and then laid into me. I tried as hard as I could to take it, while all the time chatting to the children as if everything was all right and this was somehow normal. I probably didn't fool anyone.

In those days there were very few refuges for women and kids like there are now. The police weren't particularly interested in wife-beaters – there was still the attitude that men had the right to 'chastise' their wives – and in Australia, boy, we love our 'macho' men! There was also a very real culture of victim-blaming. If you were getting beaten by your husband or boyfriend, then you probably weren't a very good wife or girlfriend and somehow deserved it. In the 1960s, the type of work available to women, and the pay they received, was far below that of men. You might want to report your bloke to the police, see him prosecuted and banged up in jail, but he was usually the breadwinner. If you had kids, what would you do then?

To complicate things even further, Michael was a complete chameleon. Sometimes he could be so lovely, he could charm the birds out of the trees. It was confusing and bewildering and scary; you never knew where you stood. I threw him a party for his twenty-first birthday, made lots of food, laid it all out, invited a few of his friends around and dressed the kids up in their finest. We sat around waiting for him for hours. When he eventually turned up, he took one look at us, seized an axe from the front yard, and smashed it down on the cake, then started hacking at the table.

The children were screaming and his friends fled as he strode around the flat demolishing pretty much everything in sight. He then went downstairs and broke all the windows of the car. He was a total madman.

Another time, I heard rumours he was seeing other women and confronted him about it. He denied it so quickly, I knew it was true and the battering I got that night – out of guilt, I felt sure – was monstrous. The next day, he turned up with a fifteen-year-old girl and hit me when I tried to stop them leaving. Afterwards, I discovered my wedding ring, and another ring I owned, were both missing.

I was angry and sad and relieved, all at the same time. It was May 1967 and it wasn't just me in a state of turmoil; it felt like the whole country was. We were sending more troops to Vietnam and sentiment was now building against our involvement, while the White Australia Policy – where non-whites previously had to be 'highly-qualified' or 'distinguished' to be allowed in – was being slowly dismantled with more Asian immigration. In addition, there was a national referendum being held on whether Aboriginal and Torres Strait Islander people should be counted in the census and be subject to Commonwealth laws, rather than just state laws. Before that, states decided on their status, which led to huge differences in their rights. For instance, they could own property in NSW and South Australia, but not in other states. They said if the federal government could make laws for them, it was likely their lot would be much improved. I thought back to my mates in Cobar and was proud to vote 'yes' in the referendum. Happily,

I was in the majority: around 91 per cent of the country voted the same way.

I didn't see Michael again until my next baby was due. He appeared out of nowhere on 16 June, the very day I started having labour pains. Presumably his dad had phoned him and he said he'd come to take me to hospital. I wasn't in any position to refuse but his car broke down on the way there, and he started shouting and hollering until we managed to stop another car and he sweet-talked the driver into giving us a lift. My second son Philip was born later that day. When Michael cradled him in his arms, I allowed myself to dare to dream that this might be a turning point for us. Now that two of my four children were his, perhaps he'd settle down and life would be less manic.

'Keep your hand under his head,' I cautioned as Michael went to put Philip down in his cot.

'I know, I know,' he said. 'You don't need to tell me.'

And then he turned and whacked me across the face. The doctors called the police. When they turned up, they marched him out of the hospital, but no one even suggested charging him. Domestic violence, back then, was just an accepted part of a woman's lot.

Chapter Seventeen
Losing Innocence

It's hard to believe I was such a fool, but Michael was a practised trickster. I was putty in the hands of someone so expert at duping people.

Wherever I ran, he'd find me and appear on the doorstep with a hangdog expression and a promise to change his ways. He'd somehow manage to charm whomever might be sheltering me and the kids into giving us back or, if that failed, he'd threaten them until they complied. He'd turn up with new cars, or a smart suit, or people who looked like gangsters, and you just knew he was up to no good but you could never quite put your finger on what was wrong. He always seemed to be doing shady deals and talking about 'acquiring' stuff – which I suspected meant stealing it – and reselling it. He'd be flush with cash one day and hand you a wad, then the next day he'd be broke and demand you give it all back.

He'd behave abominably, but then promise you the world. And I'd believe him every time, so badly did I want it to be true.

He was also always insisting we move on, to the point where I started wondering if people might be after him. We went to Broken Hill in the NSW outback, where he worked in another car yard. We went to Eulo in the Queensland outback doing odd jobs, then travelled around Western Australia, where he'd fix fences and make traps for wild horses and I'd cook and clean for people. Then we doubled back to NSW where we stayed on the south coast and he picked up more work with a mate he knew who had a sales business. But no sooner had we settled down than we'd be back on the road.

We went to South Australia, driving across the vast, empty Nullarbor Plain where we had fourteen flat tyres and broke down so many times I was terrified we'd be stranded and die there in the middle of nowhere. Michael was grim-faced and nasty the whole time, and the kids and I stayed quiet out of fear of provoking him. When we got to the other end, we picked up rocks for owners clearing land for their farms or houses. But soon we were back to Victoria, where we did some fruit picking. In one place, an elderly man whose house we stayed in berated Michael for being a wife-basher, so he retaliated by stealing two wheels off the old man's truck and selling them to someone out of town.

He was sly and smart and could be terribly vindictive. I'd started losing my innocence with Colin, but with Michael I lost it completely. He seemed to have connections everywhere. When I was stopped by the police for driving without a licence, he had a word with a mate of a mate who knew someone. Lo and behold, I suddenly had a licence.

We landed in the Melbourne suburb of Dandenong, 30 kilometres outside the city centre, and rented a house, but Michael would disappear for days at a time, leaving us without food or money. I'd walk into town with all the kids and then traipse round until I found a shopkeeper kind enough to cash my pension cheque so we could eat. Michael would then come home and act surprised that I was angry because the kids were going without. I'd get a few backhanders to boot, and a few more when he found out what I'd done with my cheque. He said he had to work late, so had no alternative to staying in town the night and eating at the local pub. I imagined he'd been with a woman too.

Sometimes, he appeared oblivious to me and the children. Other times, he became outraged when anyone else paid me any attention, acting like a jealous husband. On one occasion he ripped a new dress off me that a girlfriend had bought and shredded it with his bare hands. He'd ignore the kids, then act as though his two sons were at the centre of his world, playing with them and buying them special presents.

A few days before Christmas 1969, I discovered I was pregnant again. Although the circumstances were far from ideal, I was delighted. I'd always wanted lots of children; in a perfect world, I'd have six. I'd been so lonely as a child and longed for brothers and sisters, so I wanted to give my kids a family of their own so they could look after each other if anything ever happened to me.

By now, Debbie was seven and still as sweet and sunny-natured as she'd been the day she was born, a beautiful girly girl who loved pretty dresses and sequins and fairy stories. Linda was the polar opposite. She was nearly five, but already a tomboy. Put a nice dress on her and she'd immediately ruin it climbing a tree or playing in the mud. She'd inherited my asthma and that made me very protective, which she always tried to shrug off.

The boys were different again. Kevin was three and a half and much naughtier than my daughters had ever been, but he still liked to withdraw sometimes and play with his colouring books. I felt sure he'd grow up to be a bookworm. And Philip, at eighteen months, was up and into everything, already developing into something of a rebel.

I encouraged them to play together, for the older ones to care for the younger ones, and to sit and chat, and I did as much with them as I had time for. I'd insist on us all saying our prayers together morning and night, I'd sit and read to them, I'd make them little toys with sticks and stones and encourage them to use their imaginations. I was constantly telling them how much I treasured them. They might not have had a lot of material things, but I was determined they'd always be surrounded by love. And although Michael whacked me, he never touched the kids. If he'd done that, I'd have been off like a shot and would never have allowed him to come near us again.

As for this latest pregnancy, I couldn't tell whether he was pleased or not. I knew it was getting harder for him all the time to suddenly decide we were going somewhere else, and then pile us all in the car to head to pastures new. With the kids growing up fast, and Linda about to start school, I was keen to put down some kind of roots. The private detective had called me and said he felt he was getting closer. I really didn't want to do any more moonlight flits and risk missing whatever he unearthed, as soon as he unearthed it.

Michael spent a few days mulling over the baby news, then announced he was taking the boys on a trip to Shepparton. He had some business there and thought it would be good to have their company. But there was something in his tone that made me uneasy. I was so used to him taking off and disappearing, I was suddenly scared that he might be planning to vanish again, this time taking Kevin and Philip with him.

'Let's all go,' I suggested. 'It's about time we went on a family outing.'

He scowled. 'No, I've got to do some business there.'

'But I can look after the kids while you do your business. If you have the boys with you, that's going to make it difficult.'

'I thought it'd be good for me and the boys to spend some time together,' he said, plainly annoyed.

I wouldn't give in. 'Yes, it'd be nice for us all to spend some time together. What time should we leave in the morning?'

That night, I made sure to sleep with one eye on the boys' room to check that he wasn't stealing them away. But by the time I got up, Michael had already left – alone.

He was away all that day and night, and then early the next morning the landlord came and knocked on the door.

'I'm sorry, I have some bad news for you, Dianne,' he said. 'The police called. There's been an accident. Michael's been hurt.'

'Oh no!' I said. 'How bad is it? What kind of accident?'

'He's going to live, don't worry about that,' the landlord said kindly. 'But he was putting water in his radiator when a truck hit the back of his trailer. It pushed the car and trailer 180 feet up the road. Michael was underneath.'

'So … is he okay?' I asked.

'Apparently he's a bit of a mess. He's lost one eye and they think he might lose the other. He's at the Royal Melbourne. I'd imagine you might want to get up there straight away.'

I quickly dressed the kids and, because Michael had the car, we hitchhiked to the hospital. When I explained to the first driver who picked us up what had happened, he insisted on driving us right to the front door. All I could think, all the way there, was thank God the boys hadn't gone with Michael. They would most certainly have died that day.

Michael was discharged from hospital two weeks later with, thankfully, his other eye intact. I went with the kids to pick him up in a friend's car. I was driving us home when suddenly he lunged at me. The kids were screaming in the back. I tried to push him away with my elbow.

'What are you doing?' I yelled, trying to keep the car straight and slowing down at the same time. 'You idiot. You could get us both killed.'

'I don't care,' he said. 'It's all your fault. You should have told me not to go to Shepparton.'

'What? You wanted to go. Nothing I'd have said could have stopped you.'

By the time we arrived home, he'd worked himself up into a rage. The kids were terrified, and I tried to calm them down, and then shut them in the girls' bedroom.

As soon as the door was closed, Michael came at me again, this time grabbing my face, trying to press his fingers into my eye. It felt like he was trying to rip it out of its socket.

'I've lost mine, now it's your turn!' he bellowed.

I put one hand over my face and tried to push him back with the other. I felt overwhelmed with anger and I'm sure my eyes darkened again. I saw a milk bottle on the fridge. I picked it up and smashed it over his head. He slumped to the ground, and I saw my opening. I knew from past experience if I didn't get away fast, he'd pick up a worse weapon and retaliate. He would never, as he'd yelled at me so many times, allow a woman to get the better of him. I grabbed the kids and we ran out to the road and waved down a passing car. The driver took us into the city and we stayed there a few days until Michael tracked us down yet again.

*

That miserable pattern continued over many homes in many places until, finally, I got my lucky break. Michael had made me come with him at night to help cannibalise some trucks that were dumped near the railway line. He planned to sell the scrap metal to dealers. I was carrying a sheet of steel when we felt the ground beneath our feet start to vibrate and saw the bright light of a train bearing down on us. There was shouting and screaming and we scrambled off the tracks, just in time. But while Michael and I escaped with our lives, he lost his liberty. He was arrested, charged and convicted not only of the theft, but also of a string of fraud charges for a number of insurance rackets he'd been running.

His dad Alfred was arrested not long afterwards. Unbeknown to me, he'd been getting a gang of kids – including my Debbie and Linda – to go down to the train tracks to help him steal tonnes of steel sleeper and fish plates, worth $20,000, which he then sold for scrap. He pled guilty to 131 charges. The newspaper wrote him up as some sort of modern-day Fagin.

With Michael behind bars, I started to feel safe again. Until I noticed I was being followed. Men would suddenly appear out of nowhere and shadow me and the kids as we walked down the street. As soon as we went in the front door, they would slink off. It scared me at first, then irritated me. I was driving Debbie and Linda to school one day with the other kids in the car – by now I was six months pregnant – when I noticed a car following us. I took a few turns to make sure we were being tailed, then stopped suddenly in the middle of the road. Something in me just snapped. I got out of the car, walked up to his window and rapped sharply on it. The driver wound it down.

'What do you think you're doing?' I asked the man. 'Are you following me?'

His face went red and he looked as if he didn't know what to say.

'Tell me!' I demanded. 'Who are you? Can't you see I've got a car full of kids?'

He opened his door and climbed out. 'I'm sorry, Mrs O'Brien. But I'm with some men your Mr Brown was working with.'

'Ah, you're with the mob, then?' I said. I noted with satisfaction that he reddened even more. 'So why are you following me?'

'Well, we were told to keep tabs on you to see if you were involved in any of his, um, business ...'

'Me?' I exclaimed. 'When would I have time to be involved in his *business*? It's hard enough keeping our heads above water with four children to look after – and six months pregnant with the next – let alone be conducting a criminal business on the side!'

At that, I saw the corners of his mouth twitch, and then he laughed.

'Yes, you're right,' he said. 'I'm really sorry, Mrs O'Brien. We won't be following you anymore.'

'That's good,' I said, and turned on my heel.

That evening, a huge hamper of food was left on our doorstep. A card said it was with best wishes to me and my family. Even better, I received a phone call from the private detective. He'd found the name of my birth mother.

Chapter Eighteen
A Family Daydream

My mother's name, my *real* mother's name, was Esme Violet
Gibson. Her maiden name was Boys. Gibson ... Boys ... I racked
my brains to remember if I'd ever come across anyone with those
surnames. I felt sure I hadn't. And Esme Violet. What lovely names!
I wrote them down on a piece of paper, over and over, until they
became so familiar to me, it seemed like I'd always known them.
The excitement welled up inside. After all this time I was finally
getting close to finding my birth family.

I wondered how the detective had managed to find out her
name. Perhaps he'd tracked down Colin O'Brien and got him to ask
Dad for the adoption certificate. Colin and Dad had always been
close. Then again I couldn't believe Dad would have gone out of
his way to help a detective who was helping me.

I wanted my real dad to be a lovely, soft, kind man, a white version of someone like Jimmy Little. I wondered if they even existed. I hadn't met many so far, except for perhaps my old blood brother Brian and my first love Keith. Keith had apparently turned into a real womaniser, so he wasn't such a great role model. Brian, though, had always been there for me. Although we hadn't seen much of each other in the past ten years, we were still regularly in contact, by letter and phone. But I knew, however nice my birth mother might turn out to be, I'd never want her to replace Mum.

I found myself daydreaming about her constantly. Did she have a lot of children, like the big family I'd always longed for? How wonderful it would be for my kids to suddenly discover they had a ready-made family, with a grandmother and aunts and uncles, and even cousins. I hugged the thought close, and my dreams closer.

A couple of weeks later, the detective called me again to say he thought he'd uncovered my real name at birth. I held my breath, but I could barely contain my excitement. 'Was it Gibson?' I asked him. 'Or Boys?'

'It was … neither,' he replied. 'Your birth name was Caroline Mann.'

'Mann?' I repeated, puzzled. 'Where did that come from?'

'I'm sorry, I don't know. Maybe your father?'

'But if Mum's name was Gibson and her maiden name was Boys … I guess perhaps she wasn't married to my father?'

The detective sounded thoughtful. 'Yes, I suppose so. It's hard to say for sure until we find out more.'

I didn't have much time to continue the search. Four days after I turned twenty-four, in July 1970, I received my very best birthday present: my fifth child, a little girl I called Cindy. She was small, weighing only 5 pounds, and after the doctor delivered her, he took her away for tests. The next day, he said they believed her brain may have been starved of blood during the birth and we should keep a close eye on her. He also told me that she'd had a twin who hadn't developed, probably because I was suffering from malnutrition after so many years of trying to survive on nothing. I also had a fibroid in my tube and would have to have one of my ovaries taken out which would mean I wouldn't be able to have any more kids.

I was sad; I'd always wanted six, but I agreed. I was naturally worried about Cindy, too, but when I took her home, the other kids were so excited. Debbie, now eight, was like a mini-mum. Whenever I let her, Debbie would carry Cindy around, talking to her as if she were her very best playmate. Linda would then often beg for a turn, but Debbie would only agree after giving precise instructions on how her little sister was to be held. The boys, now four and three, were vaguely interested, but much preferred playing together.

It was a fun time for us all. Michael was safely away in jail and I was earning a living collecting people's old clothes, bringing them back to the house, sorting them with the help of the kids – sometimes – then selling them at the factory.

Some friends suggested I rent a cheaper place that was coming up nearby. The decision was made for me by the kids. They'd been playing in a shed packed with straw bales right next door to our house, and one evening I looked out of the window to see flames leaping from the shed's openings. I raced over, but luckily all the children were standing outside, looking wide-eyed at the fire. I never found out what happened, but I suspect they'd been playing with matches. Happily, the owner wasn't too bothered and assumed one of his workers had dropped a lit cigarette.

The new house wasn't far away. Around this time my friend Brian got in touch and said a friend of his, Robert Horne, was coming to work in the area. Did I want a boarder? The extra money would definitely help, since I had five mouths to feed now, so I agreed. Robert was a good bloke, and was great with the children. They took an instant liking to him and I was pleased that at last they had a man in their life who might set a good example. In time, one thing led to another and he asked if he could take me out. I agreed.

Robert was very different to Colin and Michael. He never raised his voice and never threatened me. He was gentle with the kids and got on well with them all. Everyone was happy. Then he asked if I'd consider moving to the small town of Yarragon, where his family lived, close by the Moe River in West Gippsland. We went over to have a look when Cindy was five months old, and I agreed. They had a lovely old house there, with lots of room for all of us. My Uncle Ken and Aunty Peg came to live at Poowong, another little town nearby, to be close to us, and it was wonderful to be surrounded by so much family.

We all settled down quickly and, for the first time since my mother had died, I actually felt safe. Perhaps too safe. I'd been told after I gave birth to Cindy that I couldn't have more children, but the doctor was wrong. Seven months after we moved to Yarragon, I was pregnant again. I was surprised, but pleased. I'd always wanted six children. Even better, Robert was over the moon.

Life was good and not even Michael Brown could spoil it. At least not through lack of trying. He tracked us down by ringing all the schools in the region to see where my kids were. Stupidly, I'd registered them under the surname 'Brown' when he was with us to keep it simple. I should have thought to change it when he went to jail, when we were suddenly free. But Robert stood up to him. He said he could visit his kids, but that I was with him now, and the other children were with him, and Michael couldn't see them or try to take any of the kids away. They were staying put.

It was an unusual show of strength from Robert, and I admired him for it, and was grateful, especially when Michael slunk away, defeated. But in other ways, I found Robert difficult. I'd been brought up with so much violence, I found it hard coping with a nice guy. It sounds ridiculous, even as I write it. But I honestly didn't know anything different. I couldn't help seeing his kind nature as some sort of weakness.

'You grew up being abused,' Uncle Ken said to me one day. 'Then you had two men who bashed you so badly, you got used to it.'

'I guess so.'

'So now you won't believe anyone loves you unless they love you enough to hit you when they're mad.'

'Maybe.'

'But come on, Dianne. You've got a lovely bloke there in Robert. Don't stuff this up.'

And I tried, I really did. But I found Robert kind of wet, and so nice he could be irritating. He was also pretty careless with some of the things I valued. I'd saved up my child endowment payments for years and bought myself a new Holden HD station wagon – my first ever new car – to make it easier getting around with the kids. Robert borrowed it, took it kangaroo-shooting, had an accident and smashed it up. I was devastated.

'Oh come on, Di, it's only a car!' he said airily as I looked in horror at the damage.

'But it's *my* car, and I saved and saved for it. And it was perfect.' I found it hard to forgive him.

'I'll see if the car yard has something going cheap,' he said. 'We only need something to get around town.'

That wasn't the point. I'd been so happy and proud of my new Holden and he really didn't even sound sorry.

Since childhood, I'd always kept a spotlessly clean house, like Mum had taught me. That was important. But Robert could be so slovenly and messy, it sometimes felt like I was spending all my time cleaning up after him. He'd spent his youth being followed around by his mum, making sure everything was perfect, and hadn't learnt many domestic skills. For me, it was hard enough keeping everything tidy with five kids; I didn't need a grown-up one who should have known better. He always promised he'd try harder, but I don't think he really meant it.

I also missed Sydney and I was impatient to get back and start trying to trace my birth family. Was Esme Violet still living in NSW? Why had she given me up? Had she not wanted me, or had

I been taken, just like my own daughter Debbie was so nearly taken from me at Crown Street? And what about my real dad? Was he still alive? I was impatient to find out but I couldn't do much while I was stuck in Victoria, and I knew Robert wouldn't want to leave his mum and the rest of his family now we were all living so close.

In mid-December 1970, my old blood brother Brian came to visit. It was a welcome distraction. We'd stayed in touch but I hadn't actually seen him for years. I was pleased to catch up with him again, but he'd changed. He was now married but I'd heard he hit his wife and drank too much. But it was still good to see someone who'd known me forever. One day when he and Robert were out somewhere, something very, very strange happened.

The drinks man used to come around the houses in summer with a big box of cool drinks. He regularly called at our place, and I'd buy drinks for me and the kids. This day was very hot, and I was eight months pregnant and I was feeling the heat even more than usual. The man carried the drinks into the kitchen for me, then put them down, turned round and suddenly slammed me up against the wall, pushing his body against mine. At first I was bewildered. I didn't know what he was trying to do and I was so heavily pregnant, I could barely move. When I realised he was trying to rape me, I felt for a weapon and my hand closed over a kitchen knife on the counter. I picked it up and then held it at the back of his neck and said I'd use it if he didn't get off me. He couldn't get out of my house fast enough.

I was so shocked, I couldn't stop shaking. It brought back so many memories of the first time I was raped by that thug in

173

Granville, and then by Colin, and then by my old schoolfriend's brother when I was pregnant with Linda. What was it with men and pregnant women? I sank to the ground and sat there for ten minutes, trying to recover my composure. The encounter really threw me. When Robert came home later that afternoon, he was horrified. But, God help me, I couldn't help comparing him to Colin. When I was with Colin, everyone was so scared of him – me included, I had to admit – that no one would dare touch me.

Robert called his brother and they went out together to look for the drinks man. He asked Brian to stay and look after me. We settled down for our first big chat without Robert present and straight away he asked me how things were going with us two. I said okay, but that I found Robert a bit weak, somehow. Then I started telling him about the drinks man and how he'd tried to assault me. As I talked, the tears started rolling down my cheeks.

Brian pulled me into a hug and held me tight as I wept, making soothing noises.

'You know I've always loved you, Di,' he said. 'Ever since those first days at school.'

'Yes, and I've always loved you, too,' I replied, pulling away and blowing my nose.

'No Di, I mean I *really* loved you.'

I stared at him. What was he saying? I tried to laugh it off.

But then he grabbed my shoulders. 'But you never let me be your boyfriend, did you?'

I tried to shake him off. This felt so weird. I wondered if he'd been drinking. 'We were always good friends,' I said, laughing, trying to change the mood. 'We had some good times together … Remember when we used to collect all those damned bottles?'

'You're not listening to me, Di,' he said, more urgently this time, and not letting go. I could feel his fingers digging into my shoulders and I suddenly felt sick. No, this couldn't be happening. Not with Brian. Not with my old blood brother. Not with the boy I'd grown up with, who knew more about me than anyone else in the world. I'd never seen him like this before.

I tried to stand up and ease myself out of his hold. But I was eight months pregnant and it was hard enough to stand at the best of times, without a large man pushing me back on the lounge. 'No, Brian!' I screamed. 'No! Let me go! I'm pregnant! Think of the baby! Stop!' I started hitting his chest and trying to pull at his hair but he just pushed me harder and then clambered on top of me.

It was the most devastating experience of my life. As kids, we'd mixed our blood. We'd sworn to be friends forever more. It was far more shocking than anything else I'd ever been through.

I wondered if somehow I was giving off an air of vulnerability, like I did in the early days when I was young. Was it because I was with Robert? Did that contribute to it in any way? Robert was Brian's friend, too. To this day, I've never been able to get over that sense of betrayal.

*

My third son, and sixth child, David, was born, thankfully unharmed, on 12 January 1972. He was a huge baby – weighing 10 pounds, twice Cindy's weight – and incredibly needy. He was hungry all the time. I was exhausted looking after him, the other kids, and Robert. Eighteen-month-old Cindy in particular needed special attention and the day before had cried her heart out when she saw rain for the first time. I think she thought the sky was falling down and the world was about to end. I wanted to go back to Sydney. I wanted to be back in familiar places among people I knew and, most of all, I wanted to find out about my real parents and family.

I put my name down for a Housing Commission house in Sydney's western suburbs and settled down for the wait. I spent every spare moment daydreaming about the time when I could go back and search for my real family and finally make contact with Esme Violet, wherever she might be, her husband and, hopefully, all my brothers and sisters.

PART THREE
FOUND

Chapter Nineteen
A Fresh Lead

Three years later, in 1975, I was allocated a Housing Commission house. I was overjoyed – Robert markedly less so – but we packed up everything and, with the car fit to bursting with so many kids and possessions, made our way back over the border. The house was a four-bedroom weatherboard in Terra Nova Place in Tregear, about 35 kilometres west of the CBD, near Mount Druitt. It was a real battlers' suburb that had just been developed by the NSW Department of Housing. But it was good enough for us.

While the house was being made ready, we stayed in a caravan in a friend's backyard. I found a job doing night shifts in a plastics factory, which was really well paid, and Robert got a great position at the tyre producers Goodyear Australia. For the first time in my life we were making decent money. And we were happy – or at least I thought we were. Robert had trouble settling down in Sydney and kept saying how much he missed his mum and his family. I brushed it off and told him once he got used to it, he'd love it as much as I did. I was wrong. One day, he went off to work and just never came home. That evening, he phoned me from Victoria, saying he'd been homesick, had gone back to live with his folks, and there was nothing I could say or do to persuade him to return.

I was sad, but philosophical. I had enough going on with the children and their school and my work to worry too much about him. We moved into our new house and, with my wages, I could finally afford decent food, some nice clothes, and whatever the kids wanted. Debbie was twelve and loved nice dresses; Linda, eleven, was happiest with jeans and t-shirts; Kevin, nine, was such a bookworm, he just wanted books and comics; Philip, eight, loved his toy cars; five-year-old Cindy was still into dolls; and David, even at the tender age of three, had a real artistic flair and loved nothing more than butcher's paper and colouring pencils. It was wonderful being able to take them to the zoo and for picnics, all the kinds of things we'd never been able to do before.

Occasionally, Keith would drop by to visit Linda, and Michael would call in to see his three. I'd usually stay well out of the way when they were there. I managed to track down my half-brother Ronnie and he welcomed me back with open arms and was thrilled to meet my kids. He told me that, as well as trying to get me out of the cells in Parramatta Police Station where they'd taken me when Dad was on holiday, he'd also tried to get me out of the terrible Parramatta Girls Home. He'd told Dad I could come to live with him when I got out, but Dad never passed that message on, leaving me with Colin O'Brien as my only option.

*

At the age of twenty-nine, I was diagnosed with cancer of the cervix. I had a major operation, where the doctors removed my remaining ovary, my tubes and womb. The operation went well, I was given the all-clear, but I was told I couldn't have any more kids. I know it sounds crazy, but I'd daydreamt about having twelve and was sad my childbearing years were over. I guess it was a result of having no real family of my own anymore. I wanted to surround myself with the love of a big crowd of kids instead. But I knew I was lucky to have three girls and three boys.

I also had a bit more time on my hands to try to trace my real family. Every lead I'd followed so far had come up blank, so I decided to start at the beginning. Just after my thirtieth birthday, I left the kids with some friends and drove to Wagga Wagga to visit the hospital where I'd been told I was born. I hoped that bit, at least, was true.

I enjoyed the drive there, stopping for a sandwich that I ate gazing over the Murrumbidgee River that runs close by the town. Then I took a deep breath and went to the hospital and asked to see the supervisor. He invited me into his office and I said I'd like to see the book that contained all the births at the hospital.

He gestured to a chair on the other side of his desk, took a seat himself and shook his head. 'I'm sorry, Mrs O'Brien. All our records were destroyed in the floods of 1974. You probably heard about them. Five floods. The river was so high that year. The water in town was nearly 9 metres. It was an horrendous time for the town.'

I must have looked ashen-faced at that because he stopped and his face softened. 'Tell me, why do you want to see the records?'

'I was adopted and I still don't know who I am. I've been trying to find out for years, but with no luck. I think my name was originally Caroline Mann, but I want to make sure.'

'Your adoptive parents didn't . . .?' he started.

'No,' I said. 'They never told me. Mum – I mean my adoptive mum – is dead now, and Dad doesn't want to have anything to do with me. This was my last hope.'

He shook his head. 'That must be terrible for you.'

'Yes, it is. It's terrible not knowing who you are, even whether your real parents are still around. I've got six kids and I'd love to be able to tell them who they are, too. But the longer this is taking me, the more I'm afraid I might be running out of time.' I felt tears well up in my eyes and he handed me a tissue. 'Maybe I'll end up never knowing,' I whispered.

'That'll never do,' he said. 'Tell me, what year was it again that you were born? I'll go down into the archives just on the off-chance we might still have that year's register.'

'Thank you. I'd really appreciate that.'

He left the office and was away so long, I wondered if he'd done a runner, hoping I'd give up and leave him be. But after three-quarters of an hour or so, he came back in with a huge grin on his face and a big red book under his arm.

'We're in luck!' he said, putting the book down on the desk with a thud. 'Now, let's have a look. July the third, you thought?'

I stood up and joined him behind the desk as he ran a finger down the list of names. 'No ... no ...' he said. 'Are you *sure* you were born here?'

'Yes. Definitely. Is there no one there by that name?'

'Well, there was a baby born that day called Mann, but he was a boy. That can't be you.' I felt my heart sink. 'The baby girl born on that day was called ... Caroline Governor.'

'Caroline Governor,' I repeated. 'I guess that must be me. Now I'm even more confused than I was before!'

After leaving the hospital, I went to the Births, Deaths and Marriages office in Wagga Wagga to see if I could find the birth certificate of either Caroline Mann or Caroline Governor. But under the *Welfare Act*, I was told I could only be given the birth certificate of Dianne Westman. I could have screamed with frustration.

*

I wasn't sure where to look next and dithered over what to do. Some days, I thought I should just give up. Apart from Mum, the family I knew hadn't brought me much happiness. Would my real family be any different? Why had Esme Violet given me away? Did she not love me? What if I found her and the rest of the family and they didn't want to know?

Christmas that year came and went, and then the terrible news of the Granville rail disaster broke in January 1977. A train derailed and hit the supports on a road bridge that then collapsed onto the carriages, killing eighty-three and injuring more than 213 people. I went over to Granville as a gesture of solidarity. The railway line was a hive of activity, but the rest of the suburb was under a pall of gloom. Luckily, none of my friends had been involved, but it seemed everyone knew someone who'd been affected. So many people were in mourning.

*

A few months later, I heard about a new organisation that had just started up called Jigsaw, helping people who'd been adopted. They worked with people with happy lives, people with tragic lives, and those, like me, who were still searching for their birth parents. They told me there'd been 140,000 to 150,000 adoptions in the period between 1951 and 1975, and a lot of those were forced. I knew all about that, having so nearly had my own first-born, Debbie, stolen from me. I was interviewed by a counsellor and told they'd do their best to help me find my real parents. I was overjoyed. At last, I was getting closer.

In my own neighbourhood, I'd begun doing my bit for lost kids, too. Tregear was full of battlers back then, and the kids were often the unwitting victims. Sometimes I'd find children running wild on the streets while their parents were at work, so I'd take them in, give them a feed and make sure they were safe. I constantly had a big pot of stew on the stove to feed the hungry. Soon, people around the neighbourhood started calling me 'Black Mama'. I didn't think I was very black at all, but I guess in the children's eyes I was Italian or Greek or Lebanese or Aboriginal. I just loved helping and emulating the way my mum used to help everyone when I was young.

One time, I was in the pub with some friends and I saw a young mum balancing a baby on her knee. She was obviously drunk and my heart stopped every time I saw her lean forward and nearly drop the child. In the end, I went and gently lifted up the baby and said I'd look after her. I went to the shops, bought some baby clothes and took her home. That baby was with me for three weeks before her mum came looking for her. She phoned and we arranged to meet back in Granville – but she never showed up. Four months later, she contacted me again and said her boyfriend's mother wanted to take care of the baby. I said if the boyfriend's mother wanted her, she'd have to come and see me so I could check. When she arrived at my door, she turned out to be someone I knew from Cobar!

On another occasion, five children hammered on my door, telling me their house was on fire. I raced over there and discovered the fridge was alight, and put it out with an extinguisher. A while later, I was walking past a half-burnt-out building and heard a cry. It might have been a stray cat but I thought I'd better check. There was no one around, so I walked into the house and found a baby lying on a bed. It was ghostly white and seemed half-dead, so I took him immediately to Mount Druitt Hospital. A few days later, the police came to my house and said no one had claimed the baby, and would I look after him while they continued to search for his mother? That baby, Jake, was with me for the next fifteen months until he was finally returned to his parents. But a month later, he was back again. His parents had seven children and were drinkers and had left him locked in the car on a hot day while they were at the pub. I looked after him for another six months until they'd persuaded the courts they could be fit and proper parents again. After that, Jake's parents brought him back regularly to visit his 'second mother'. We stayed in touch till he turned twenty-one.

Yet, even as I was helping kids and their parents out, and trying to find mine, other parts of my life began to unravel. I'd been introduced by Ronnie's partner Maggie to a man at the annual Granville Ball. He seemed to have a lot of money, but he'd been drunk at the time and dropped his wallet. I'd picked it up and, just for a moment, thought about keeping it so I could take the kids out somewhere nice, rather than watch him blow it all on grog. But, of course, I couldn't. He was delighted when I returned his wallet and asked me out. We then started seeing each other.

Don Reid was a bit older than me, a divorcé with three sons, one of whom had undergone an operation to become a woman. He was a nice man and the kids all liked him, which was always the most important thing. After a while, he moved in with us and became very much the father they'd never had. He was firm with them, but fair. They had to eat all their dinner before they left the table, they had to say please and thank you, and each do a share of the jobs around the house. Don drew up a roster for household chores and got us all organised. He wanted to look after us. He was just as at home chatting with Debbie and Linda about their favourite pop stars as he was playing football with the boys in the backyard. When Linda fell pregnant at the age of just fourteen and had twin boys, he was as supportive of her as he was of me.

We'd always been protective of Cindy, who was seven by then but still young for her age. It had been confirmed she'd sustained brain damage at birth, but she was still a bright and happy child. Don had a real soft spot for her, and was very patient and caring.

We were at home one afternoon when David tore into the house shouting that someone was trying to hurt Cindy. He'd run all the way home from school in a panic to let us know. I immediately dashed out of the house, but Don beat me to it. He arrived at the school to hear that a sixteen-year-old boy had attacked Cindy and tried to rape her. A security guard had heard her screams and come and wrested the boy off her – just in time. Cindy was shaking and crying in the corner, with her teacher trying to calm her down. The police were on their way.

Cindy wasn't badly hurt physically, but overnight she went from a sunny little thing to a quiet, withdrawn girl with a haunted look in her eyes. She was a completely different kid. Sometimes she'd wet her bed and she no longer wanted to wear pretty dresses or have her hair styled. She would only wear the dowdiest and most shapeless of clothes, making herself as unattractive as possible as it seemed to make her feel safer. It tore at my heart to see her like that, and Don was devastated too that he hadn't been able to keep her out of harm's way.

I was touched by his concern and thought again how lucky we were to have him in our lives. There was only one negative though, but it was quite a big one: he was a heavy drinker. I'd never been a drinker but now, at the age of thirty-two, I had my first beer. In the beginning, it was just to keep Don company. Then, I started trying to keep up with him and his friends. It started slowly, but over time, it insidiously crept up on me, very nearly ruining our lives.

Chapter Twenty
The Demon Drink

It was as clear as day that Don was drinking too much. Every morning I'd go round the house collecting the empties and tipping away any grog left in the bottles. One morning, it occurred to me that it was a waste of money throwing the booze out, so I decided to drink it instead. It wasn't one of my brightest decisions.

Soon after, Don and I started drinking together every weekend. We just didn't stop. Sure enough, we began arguing and our fights would get out of hand. I hated it, and we both said we'd not drink the next weekend, or the next, or the next ... but somehow we always did. I got a taste for beer and Jack Daniel's. Very soon, it got completely out of hand.

I was depressed and frustrated that I was still getting nowhere trying to find my real family. I called Jigsaw weekly at first, then monthly, but they kept saying they had nothing to report. I was losing hope. Would I ever be happy when I didn't know who I was? Could I be the best mum I wanted to be to my kids when I had no idea where I'd come from? I was lost and drifting, at risk of drowning in a lake of booze.

I went over to Granville one day to visit the Royal Hotel and was sitting there drinking with a friend when who should walk in but Colin O'Brien, my long-lost husband. He stopped dead to see me with a beer in front of me; he'd never seen me drink before. I was equally stunned to see him; it had been sixteen years since he'd left. He sat down at our table and my friend started berating him for everything he'd done to me when I was a kid. I was quiet; somehow I couldn't find it in myself to go back there. What was the point? He turned to me and asked how I was.

'Terrific,' I said.

'And the kids?'

'They're terrific, too. They've now got a great stepdad and we're all very happy.' I was pleased to see he looked pained at that. 'Our lives really are wonderful now,' I continued, rubbing it in. 'Just wonderful.'

'I'm glad, Di,' he said, looking anything but. 'Hey, do you think I could see the kids sometime?'

I wondered who he meant at first, but then remembered that, while Debbie was his, he'd always thought Linda was his too, rather than Keith's.

'I'll ask them,' I said. 'Give me your number and I'll let you know.' I never did.

A month or so later, Don happened to be at the same pub with a couple of mates and phoned me to come down. I drove over and, to my surprise, found him standing there with Colin O'Brien.

'This bloke reckons he was married to you,' Don said, laughing.

'Yes, that's right,' I said. 'And we're still married.'

The smile on his face froze. 'For real? I didn't believe him when he told me.'

'Yes, unfortunately it's true.'

After that, Colin would occasionally call round to see the children – I kept well away – but I don't think they were too enthusiastic. Secretly, that pleased me no end.

Meanwhile, Don and I carried on drinking. He started getting violent, just like Colin, but I was tougher by now, so I'd fight back if I thought I could get the upper hand. We both started using weapons, and the kids would say they'd get scared as my eyes went black. Don wouldn't just hit me in the face; he'd hit me in the face with a bottle of beer or, once, with a six-pack. I wouldn't just punch him back; I'd grab a knife or a screwdriver and stab him. Thinking about it now, it's astonishing I'm still alive and still have my front teeth. Many others in my position would be dead by now. I'm sure a lot are.

Like Colin and Michael, though, Don never went near the kids when he was drinking, otherwise I knew I would have killed him. He was still his old genial, loving self with them – someone I glimpsed less and less often now that we were drinking so much. Sober, he was the perfect partner. Drunk, he was a nightmare.

Even though he kept his distance when he was drunk, the kids couldn't help but be affected. They'd always had a mum utterly devoted to them, and had got used to Don keeping them in check, but now they started running wild. Linda moved out of home when she turned sixteen with her boys to a three-bedroom house in Bonnyrigg, 25 kilometres south of Tregear. In 1981, Debbie, who was now nineteen, had her son and moved into a house just around the corner from Linda. At the same time, Kevin, aged fifteen, changed from being a bookworm and a kid mad on watching and playing football all the time to a boy who seemed lost and always in trouble. Fourteen-year-old Philip, who'd always been a rebel, hung out with his brother, and the pair befriended a group of older boys who were up to no good. They got caught stealing and suddenly I was making regular trips to the police station and talking to solicitors in court. Even worse, David, then aged nine, was becoming more of a rebel and acting up like his big brothers. One day, he was playing with Cindy, two years older than him and always so quiet and well-behaved, when he hit her with a stick and broke her collarbone. I knew it was an accident, but it shocked me. Of course I blamed myself. How could I expect them to behave when I was acting like a madwoman?

Alcohol had taken over our family. I took to grog so enthusiastically because it was a great way to forget what had happened to me in the past, to blot out the pain. Stupidly, I didn't realise it was only making everything worse. Don and I were fighting so much, it didn't seem worth being together anymore. I still loved him and I think he still loved me, but we needed to be apart. He moved out for a while to give us a break.

One night in late 1982, Kevin hammered on the door of my

bedroom. 'Mum! Mum!' he shouted. 'There's a fire! We've got to get out!'

I leapt out of bed as if I'd been bitten by that shark that was always chasing me in my nightmares and ran to the bedroom he shared with Philip and David. I could feel the heat even before I got there, could hear the roar and could see the yellow flames in the crack under the closed door.

'Where's Philip?' I yelled over the noise. 'Where's David? Where are the girls?'

'Philip's waking them all up!' Kevin shouted back.

'Let's help him,' I said, and we raced to each of the bedrooms in turn to make sure everyone was either getting up or was already outside. David had just woken up to see his room on fire, so I rushed in, covered him in a doona and half-carried, half-pushed him out of the window.

'Go outside,' I told Kevin, 'and check everyone's there now.'

As he dashed outside, I went back to his bedroom. I opened the door a crack and there was the sound of an explosion. I slammed it quickly shut again.

Thank God all the kids were outside waiting for me. Soon the sounds of sirens echoed from up the road. Minutes later, the place was filled with firemen and trucks and hoses and an ambulance. The neighbours came out and watched our house slowly singe and crackle and warp in the heat.

After we were all checked over, we were given another house to stay in for a few weeks. I insisted, however, that we wanted to return to our old place as soon as it'd been rebuilt. I was told we were the only tenants who'd ever wanted to do such a thing. But I liked it. I thanked God that I hadn't been drinking that night and had been able to help get the kids out. I swore I would never drink again. It turned out a fuse in an electric blanket had shorted and set fire to the sheets. Luckily three of our beds were water beds, so that had helped douse the fire and meant we hadn't lost too much.

Don, bless him, came over and helped us move and, eight weeks later, helped us move back again into the newly rebuilt house. He stayed with us for a bit, but things didn't improve much. He was still drinking and I soon joined him. Every time I tried to give up, I'd dose myself up with Serepax to treat the withdrawal symptoms or smoke dope to calm me down. Soon, I was doing all three at once.

Somehow, I still managed to keep an eye on the kids. Michael Brown asked to take his sons Kevin and Philip up to Queensland for the school holidays, and they were so keen to go I didn't have the heart to refuse. When I got a call from Philip that Michael wasn't being terribly nice to them, however, I drove straight to his house, told him I was taking them back, and drove them home to Tregear again.

Eventually, the drinking and fighting got too much, and Don left for good. I was heartbroken and took an overdose, but luckily lived. If it hadn't been for the kids, I probably would have tried harder and succeeded. Then Don phoned one night and told Philip *he'd* taken an overdose. He didn't seem the type at all to carry through with such a threat. We discussed it as a family, but none of us believed him. We thought he was just saying that in the hope that I'd let him come back to live with us again, and I really didn't want him back as he'd caused us so much damage. So in the end we didn't do anything. But Don wasn't as lucky as me. His sister called the next morning to tell us he was dead.

The old saying is right: you never realise how much you're going to miss someone until they're gone. That was true of Don Reid. We were utterly crushed by his death. Cindy cried herself to sleep. Philip, who'd been seeing a girl at school, announced at age fifteen, with her just fourteen, they were having a child, and moved out to live with her and her mum.

I called Jigsaw again. Still no news.

And then something truly bizarre happened. An Aboriginal man rocked up to my front door.

'I'm Donnie Williams, the Aboriginal counsellor at your kids' school,' he explained. 'I thought I'd call around and see how you are.'

'Philip's not in any trouble, is he?' I asked immediately.

'No, not at all,' he said and laughed. 'I'd just never met his mum and wanted to say hello.'

'But why would you come here?' I asked, puzzled. 'If you're the Aboriginal counsellor, surely you just look after the Aboriginal pupils?'

It was his turn to look puzzled. 'But Philip and Cindy and David *are* Aboriginal,' he said. 'It's obvious.'

'Obvious?' I repeated stupidly.

'Well, of course. You just have to look at all of you to know that ...'

'But I don't know that,' I said, cutting him off. 'The problem is,

I don't know what I am. I don't know where I come from. I never knew my real parents. I'm sorry, my manners. Do you want to come in for a cup of tea?'

The man came in and told me that, if my kids were indeed Aboriginal, then they might qualify for a living allowance from ABSTUDY, the government scheme that encouraged black kids in their education. In return, I told him my story, and how I'd been trying to trace my birth family for years. I was now hoping that Jigsaw might be able to come up with something, but I was running out of options. He suggested I try a new organisation called Link-Up, which helped Aboriginal people who'd been forcibly removed from their mothers and fostered, adopted out, or placed in institutions.

'But I don't know if I'd qualify,' I said. 'I don't know if I'm Aboriginal. Since I found out I was adopted, I'd always thought I was Irish or Italian or Maltese, or that maybe I had a black American father.'

He looked at me for a while without speaking. 'Well, there's only one way to find out. Here's their number.'

Chapter Twenty-one
Finding Mum

It only took a few months for Link-Up to come back to me after our first meetings with a letter saying they'd found out more about my birth mother. Esme Violet Boys was born in Melbourne in 1920 and was twenty-six when she gave birth. That's when the adoptions board had written her name down as Violet Gibson. And yes, she was Aboriginal.

I was stunned both by finding out more about my real mum, and discovering, after all this time, my true identity. I had a proud heritage I could now align myself to; a living, breathing culture. All those years I'd felt different, and all that teasing I'd endured for being darker than other kids, now made sense. I'd always wanted to belong and now I'd discovered I belonged to the oldest people on earth. It felt good to know who I was, and be able to share that with my children. We'd found our place in the world.

The more I thought about it, the more it made sense. I'd always had Aboriginal friends wherever I went, like in Cobar and in La Perouse and even back in Granville. Jimmy Little had been so kind to me; I wondered if he'd seen it, too. He'd stopped performing a few years before to concentrate on teaching and community work and his family. I decided I'd look him up at the first opportunity. Then there was that very black man in Walgett who'd assured me I was Aboriginal. How could they all have known, but I didn't?

I shook my head and went back to the letter. The founders of Link-Up, Coral Edwards – who herself had been removed from her Koori family and raised in a girls' home – and Peter Read – who was researching the impacts of government policies on the Wiradjuri people of NSW – wanted to know if I'd like them to keep digging for more information. Luckily for me, they'd set up the first Indigenous family tracing and reunion service, and if I wanted to go further, all I had to do was sign the form requesting my mother's birth certificate. Grateful for their help, I signed the form straight away.

Soon after, in September 1984, I received another letter. It said that my mother's mother – my grandmother – had been born at Echuca in Victoria, about 200 kilometres north of Melbourne, on the banks of the Murray River. Like Jimmy Little, she was a proud Yorta Yorta woman, a member of the clan who lived in the river country around north-eastern Victoria and southern NSW. My mouth fell open when I read that. River people. I really was a daughter of the river country. It explained why I'd always been drawn to water, especially rivers, ever since I was a child. My family had gone to the beach but I'd always pined for the river.

Link-Up said they'd carry on with their research and let me know how they were going in due course. I was so excited, I was nearly bursting. Suddenly, my troubles didn't seem so bad. I had an identity, I had a past and now, I felt sure, I could have a future.

*

At home, I tackled my kids' problems with renewed vigour. By that stage only Kevin, Cindy and David were still living with me. At age eighteen, Kevin was a little lost. Because my own childhood had been cloaked in secrets and lies, I'd always wanted to be open and honest with my kids. I'd never hidden from him that he was a twin, but that his brother had never developed in the womb. At school, his classmates found out he'd lost a baby brother and started taunting him with a gruesome American horror film called *Basket Case*. It was about a boy who carries around his deformed twin brother who'd been born conjoined with him, but surgically separated. The pair seek vengeance on the surgeon and the deformed twin ends up trying to kill his brother. Kevin became obsessed with the film and watched it over and over again. Even worse, he'd started drinking, too.

Cindy was also having problems. She was enrolled at a special school for children with intellectual disabilities, but from the start, seemed to be going backwards. Don and I agreed to send her there at the authorities' suggestion, but in retrospect, I think she just got lost in the cracks of the system. When she was fourteen, I took her out of that school and told her she didn't have to go back. With the help of her older sisters, we'd homeschool her to give her a much better chance in life. Our efforts received a substantial boost when finally, at the age of fifteen in July 1985, she was awarded $10,000 in compensation for the attack she'd suffered at her old school. It could never make up for the trauma, but it did help to improve the quality of her life.

Aged thirteen, David was still my baby, and I told him to never get into the kind of trouble his brothers had been in. I had high hopes. But all those appearances in court I'd made, and the work I'd done with solicitors on Kevin's and Philip's behalf, did bear fruit in other ways. I made friends with the administrator of the local St Mary's Aboriginal Legal Service and she offered me a job.

'That's very kind of you to think of me, but I don't have any formal training!' I protested.

'Yes, I know that. But you have experience, and that teaches you stuff that can't be learnt in a classroom. And as we now know, you're Aboriginal, too.'

I laughed. 'But I don't know ...'

'But I do! You'll be perfect. You'll pick it up quickly and you already know your way around the court system.'

'Yes, but only as the mother of the accused,' I said. 'That's probably not the best background.'

She raised her eyebrows. 'I disagree. It's the *perfect* background. You'll know exactly how our clients will be feeling, how they'll react and what to do to help. I've seen all the voluntary work you do too, helping kids in trouble. You can't tell me this isn't something you wouldn't enjoy.'

She was right and I loved the work. It was the perfect professional extension of the one thing I adored doing most as a volunteer – helping people. I also treasured the fact that I was doing the kind of thing Mum had always done.

*

Soon after, I received more news from the people at Link-Up. It turned out I was a direct descendant of a very old, very famous and very well-respected Aboriginal family in Victoria who traced their lineage back to pre-invasion times. Moreover, the researchers had actually been to visit one of my oldest relatives, a great-aunt who was now living in a Melbourne nursing home. Through her, they'd found out that my birth mother was still alive. Next, they planned to go and visit her, show her my photo and have a chat to see if she'd be willing to see me.

I spent the next two weeks with my heart in my mouth. Every time the phone rang, I jumped. By the time Link-Up called, I was exhausted. But they had good news. While my birth mother had never told her husband or her other children about me, she had long wondered what had happened to her baby, had looked at my photo and – best of all – said she was prepared to see me. I was over the moon. After all these years, at the age of thirty-eight, I was finally going to meet my real mother.

Link-Up visited and told me not to get my hopes up too high. They said I'd have to approach my mother delicately. They warned me against asking direct questions about her life, her pregnancy, the identity of my father and my adoption, and to concentrate instead on trying to forge a bond. They recommended I show her pictures from my family album, talk about my kids – her grandkids – and give her the room to talk about anything she wanted.

When the day of our meeting dawned I was overcome with nerves. I caught the train to Parramatta where the Link-Up people met me and walked me to a nondescript café in a shopping centre. There, they introduced me to my mum, and discreetly left us. She looked just like Linda. We talked, non-stop, for five hours. She told me that when I was fifteen, she'd gone to Wagga Wagga to look for me, she'd missed me so much.

A few days later, she came round to my house and gave me a jewellery box she'd secretly bought me for my eighteenth birthday. I loved that she'd been thinking of me. But it was odd. I'd imagined I'd feel a real bond with her, but I didn't. I don't know if we'd been apart too long, or if there was too much resentment on my part, or goodness knows what on her part, but it felt like we were just friends meeting up for coffee. I didn't feel like her daughter, and she never gave me any indication that she felt like my mum.

The third time we met up, she kept talking about her new family. I was excited to learn she had five daughters so I had five half-sisters, the five sisters I'd always dreamt of! I couldn't resist asking her some direct questions, some of which she answered, others of which she deflected. I found myself getting frustrated, but I tried to hide it and stay polite. I asked her why my name had been registered as Mann or Governor and she said she'd put down the name of our cousins instead of her own. I showed her some of the photos Link-Up had given me of our ancestors and she seemed surprised that many of them were so dark-skinned. She said she hadn't known she was Aboriginal, either, until she was nineteen. When I asked about my real dad, she said he'd been ready to marry her when another woman he'd been seeing said she was pregnant and he'd gone back to her. She told me he'd since died of a heart attack. I was upset. I didn't really want to replace Mum, my adoptive mother who'd brought me up and whom I worshipped, but I would have loved to have got to know my dad. I wanted someone to replace my adoptive dad so I could wipe all memories of him.

There were some weird coincidences. Esme was Catholic and very devout, just like my adoptive parents. Most bizarrely, she'd lived for years just around the corner from us in Granville! I couldn't get over that. All that time I'd been searching for her, and she'd been so close. She then showed me a photo of her wedding, and there, standing next to her husband, was the best man – none other than Lenny McPherson. I never got a straight answer as to whether these coincidences were twists of fate, or something more meaningful ...

Esme said she'd like to meet my daughters, but strangely, she never asked much about them. Instead, she talked a lot about her own kids. Her first had been put in a boarding home and never lived with her again, but then she'd had two more, then me – all to different fathers. She'd finally had two more daughters with her current husband. When I asked if one day I'd be able to meet my half-sisters, she said they didn't know I existed and she wasn't sure she wanted to tell them. I was hurt but tried not to show it.

I was really happy at meeting my birth mother after all this time, but back home, things weren't so good. David was getting into the same kind of trouble that Kevin and Philip had been in before him, steadily accruing a police record for offences like driving without a licence and stealing motorbikes to go on joyrides. In my new position at the Aboriginal Legal Service, I was conscious it wasn't a good look and so I gave him a stern talking to, as did Debbie, who'd always been his second mum. I introduced him to the Harrisons, who gave him a couple of lessons in fighting, like they had with me so many years before, which I thought might stand him in good stead. Cindy meanwhile had her first boyfriend, but I was concerned that he didn't seem to be treating her right. And Kevin was drinking more and more. I knew how hard it was – I was still drinking too. Every time I tried to get sober, friends would insist on dragging me down the pub and buying me drinks, and it was the same with him.

One day, I had a brainwave and suggested we go to rehab. Together. He wasn't keen, but I managed to persuade him. We went to a residential clinic and checked in. After three days, I realised it was the worst possible place we could have picked. All the counsellors did was talk about alcohol and everyone there just wanted to get drunk! I vowed that if I ever ran a rehab course, I'd never mention booze. I'd talk about everything else to take addicts' minds off it. We checked out together and went on a mother-and-son bender.

Kevin's dad, Michael Brown, wasn't faring too well, either. I took one of my eight grandchildren, Debbie's eldest son, on a shopping trip to Wollongong one day and, as we drove out of town, I glimpsed a WANTED! poster pasted to a lamppost. My grandson saw it, too.

'Nanna, is that Pop?' he asked.

'No, silly,' I told him. 'It's just someone who looks like him.'

'But Nanna ...'

'No,' I insisted. 'Honestly, it's not him.'

I felt terrible lying to my own grandchild and wondered what on earth the police were chasing Michael for now. It must have been serious.

My husband Colin called round one day, too. I'd been to a solicitor to ask about getting a divorce but it seemed complicated, with so many forms to fill in. I also wanted as little to do with him as possible, so somehow I never got around to it. He'd turned up that day, however, to ask for Debbie's address, and brought with him an old friend I'd grown up with back in Granville. He was the Aboriginal kid, Greg Peckham, who went on to be a professional footie player, my old 'black tracker'. He'd managed to track me down again and simply never left. We fell hard for each other.

Every so often, I caught up with my birth mother Esme, trying to find out more about my past. One day, I couldn't stop myself asking her straight out why she'd given me up for adoption. It turned out she hadn't. Just like when I went into hospital to have Debbie, Esme had been told there was a lovely, wealthy couple who couldn't have any children who would take me and raise me as if I were theirs. Just like me, she'd said no. But then when I was born, the matron took me to the nursery – and my mother never saw me again.

I was stolen, like so many others.

Chapter Twenty-two
A Proud History

The knowledge that I was a stolen child proved strangely comforting. So many of those questions I'd been haunted by since I'd first learnt I was adopted were instantly answered. I'd probably long suffered from low self-esteem as a result of thinking my birth mother had willingly given me away; that the most important person in my life had rejected me. I'd felt disposable, worthless. Now, that hurt was replaced by a tangible pride in who I was and what I'd survived.

I'd known, from my experience of all those grieving girls at Parramatta Girls Home and the Myee Hostel, that the mothers who had their children taken away never forgot them, always thought of them, and lost a part of their heart when they were taken away. While I still didn't feel the kind of bond with my birth mother I'd hoped for, it was good to know that she had thought of me often over the years, and had tried to find me. It was reassuring. Some of that anger I'd had in me from a child began to melt.

I learnt that after taking me from Esme, the nurses at Wagga Wagga Base Hospital had given me to a wealthy doctor in Lockhart, a small town in the Riverina region of NSW about 65 kilometres west of Wagga Wagga. He, in turn, passed me on to his son – my adoptive dad, George Westman – whose wife Val couldn't have any more kids after having had Ronnie with her first husband. She yearned for another child. That made sense to me. I knew Mum had loved me very much, but perhaps Dad had never really wanted me in the first place.

Even though I was feeling better about my past, I still found my birth mother Esme frustrating. I asked her how she ended up living just around the corner from us in Granville. Had she managed to track me down so she could keep an eye on me? But she always moved the conversation on to something else. I was also curious about my birth dad. Was he Aboriginal? Why did they split up? But again Esme proved so evasive, I realised she really didn't want me to know. She loved talking about her other daughters, though, and I repeated how keen I was to meet them. As time went by, however, and we continued to meet in secret and she still hadn't told them about me, I began to wonder if it'd ever happen. It couldn't help feeling like yet another rejection.

As I delved into my ancestry further, I discovered my great-grandfather was none other than William Cooper, the famous Aboriginal activist and community leader. Born in 1860, William was one of the signatories of the legendary 1881 Maloga Petition to the governor of NSW, demanding that Aboriginal people be given tracts of their land back, or be able to rent or buy them so they could earn their own living. In 1935 in Melbourne, William helped establish the Australian Aborigines League, campaigning for a fair deal 'for the dark race', the repeal of discriminatory legislation and for programs to 'uplift the Aboriginal race'. The League even gathered – despite enormous opposition from the Commonwealth and state governments and white employers – signatures for a major petition for King George V in England asking that Aboriginal people be represented in the Australian parliament. The petition was printed in a newspaper and received in 1937 by the government – which then refused to pass it on to the king.

But William was undeterred. He had meetings with ministers and the prime minister and, despite being harassed by the police, was tireless in his efforts. He was one of the organisers of a Day of Mourning on Australia Day in 1938, the first ever national action by Aboriginal people. His 'Aborigines Sunday' later became NAIDOC [National Aborigines and Islanders Day Observance Committee] Week, celebrated annually by all Australians. He also became known worldwide as a great campaigner for human rights. In 1938, he led a delegation of the League from Footscray to the German consulate in Melbourne to condemn the persecution of the Jewish people by the Nazis. The consulate, however, refused to accept his letter. William's stand was later honoured by the Israeli government, and drew comparisons with the oppression of Australia's First Nation. After his death in 1941 at the age of eighty, his nephew Douglas Nicholls carried on the fight, which resulted in that 1967 Australian referendum I'd been so happy to vote 'yes' in.

At the same time as I was learning so much about the past, however, the future darkened. While I'd fallen hook, line and sinker for Greg, he turned out to be yet another boyfriend who was violent. I had to admit, I had terrible taste in men. My problem, I think, was that I always felt sorry for the underdogs – maybe I'd inherited that from my great-grandfather – but inevitably those underdogs always ended up biting me. Greg and I were fighting, we were drinking, and I realised I couldn't go on this way. I began thinking of moving somewhere new and making a fresh start.

By this time, only Cindy and David were still living at home. The older kids seemed to be settled, with Linda getting engaged and moving from Bonnyrigg to Mount Druitt, Debbie staying in Bonnyrigg with her baby, and Philip getting a house with his girlfriend and baby back in Granville. Kevin also got engaged to his girlfriend. They were expecting their first child and managed to get a Housing Commission home in Mount Druitt.

In June 1985 I decided to throw a big BBQ for Philip's eighteenth birthday and invited all the family round. After being surrounded by them for so long, I missed them now they were mostly grown up, and I really looked forward to family gatherings.

We were drinking and eating and chatting, and everything was going well until an old man from down the lane suddenly appeared in our yard, swinging an axe. He said someone had been pinching wood from his pile for our BBQ, and he started smashing the windows of my family's cars. As you'd imagine, all hell broke loose.

Philip's mother-in-law told the old bloke to stop, but he hit her with a chair. One of the boys then crash-tackled him. I was yelling at the kids to get off and leave him alone, and picked up the shaft of a shovel lying on the grass to wave it around at the boys. Suddenly there were sirens and the police arrived and arrested us all. We spent the night in the cells and my sons and I were charged with assault. I was mortified and decided it really was time to move away and start afresh.

*

I still had the charges hanging over my head when I was allocated a house in Corrimal, a northern suburb of Wollongong, about 90 kilometres south of Sydney. The boys had pled guilty to the charges levelled against them, and took the punishment, but I decided to fight my case. I'd been trying to stop the brawling, and hadn't contributed to it in any way.

Around this time, the St Mary's Aboriginal Legal Service asked me if I'd consider becoming a drug and alcohol counsellor for the Western Suburbs Drug and Alcohol Service in Mount Druitt. They didn't seem to mind that I was going to live in Corrimal and said it would be fine to commute. They didn't seem to mind either that I'd been addicted to drink and drugs; all the better, they said, to understand the clientele. So I stopped drinking completely, took the job and absolutely loved it. I counselled people about their addictions, talked to them about self-awareness and good choices, and taught them how to manage their emotions, their stress and even their welfare payments. I also helped out as a field worker in the local prisons and became so determined to clean up the system, I even reported a couple of local police officers whom I suspected of selling the drugs they took off dealers.

Greg moved to the house in Corrimal with me, along with Kevin, who was by now twenty-six and drinking less which pleased me no end. Sadly, he'd split up from his girlfriend and missed his little daughter Crystal terribly. He told me that the day he left, eighteen-month-old Crystal came running after him, crying, 'Wait for me, Daddy! Don't walk so fast ...' It was the hardest thing he'd ever done in his life, he said. Even worse, Crystal's mother moved houses, often without telling him, so he seemed always to be searching for his child. I knew that was hard for him to handle, and I advised him to put $2 every week into a bank account for her so, when he did eventually catch up with her, he'd have proof that he never stopped loving and thinking about her.

Not long after, my legal service was closed down because of some problems in the head office, but I barely missed a beat. I was offered a job at Aboriginal Medical Services in Wollongong, much closer to home. I was delighted to take it. Again, I was a drug and alcohol counsellor and attended court with clients, as well as teaching stress management, conducting workshops, writing funding submissions and having meetings with funding bodies, undertaking community projects and dealing with politicians and government agencies. They also gave me further training in counselling, communications, administration and becoming an HIV/AIDS peer educator.

My assault case finally went to court in late 1987 and was heard at Parramatta, the same courthouse that, twenty-six years before, had sentenced me for a stay at Parramatta Girls Home. I trembled in the dock as I remembered that. But despite arguing my innocence, I was found guilty and sentenced to two years' jail! I was incredulous. I'd always told my clients at the Aboriginal Legal Service to stay on the straight and narrow, go into rehab, clean up their act and they'd be dealt with fairly by the courts when their day came. I'd done all that, and I ended up with two years' jail. On my darkest day, I wondered if the officers I'd reported for selling drugs had had anything to do with the verdict.

I immediately lodged an appeal. But my lawyer told me it could take years, and in the meantime I had to start serving my sentence. So unfortunately I had another experience of déjà vu. In 1980, Parramatta Girls Home had been taken over by the Department of Corrective Services and turned into the Norma Parker Detention Centre for Women. So, guess what? After a spell at Silverwater Correctional Centre, I ended up back in exactly the same place where I'd been imprisoned as a fifteen-year-old. The cement slab we'd used for marching and which we'd had to clean with a toothbrush as a punishment was still there, and the cells were exactly the same. The only thing that was different was the regime – thank God! This time, there was no rape, no torture and no bashings. Instead, there was a whole host of activities for education and rehabilitation.

I wasn't taking any chances, though. I worked out who among the inmates was the prison kingpin and standover merchant. I tried to look as fierce as it was humanly possible, went straight up to her and told her I wouldn't make any trouble, and I didn't expect any trouble in return. If she wanted to take me on, she could, but I was warning her: I wouldn't back down. I'd lived so many years in institutions I knew that if people saw weakness, they'd take advantage of it, and I was determined that no one was going to make my life a misery. I'd had more than enough of that by now. The woman seemed surprised, but nodded. After that, she was nothing but nice to me. I shared a cell with one other woman, then had one to myself, and made friends by trading cigarettes for lollies. One woman I met told me she was there for almost killing her husband after putting Serepax in his dinner. I recalled the time I'd drugged Colin. There but for the grace of God, I thought to myself. Then I was moved on to Silverwater Correctional Centre to serve out the rest of my sentence.

At both institutions, I signed up for absolutely every course I could and threw myself into them wholeheartedly. While my appeal was trundling through the various levels, I decided I'd simply make the best of a bad situation. And it worked. I studied TAFE courses in law, computing, conflict resolution, life management skills and communication, and took various health, and women's health, certificates. I even started helping out the drug and alcohol worker there. She was pleased to have the benefit of my experience, on both sides of the equation. I also tried to stop the trade of drugs inside, played a role in organising the first-ever AIDS benefit concert at the prison, and successfully campaigned to have women issued with sunglasses for the time they spent in the courtyard in the blazing sun. I like to think William Cooper would have been proud.

But it was tough, I can't pretend otherwise. I missed my family dreadfully, and I was still angry about the sentence. I also didn't want my birth mother Esme to see me like this. I wanted to continue our meetings in the hope of finding out more information about my real dad, and I still wanted to meet my half-sisters.

*

Just when things seemed to be improving, my youngest son, David, was at a friend's house messing around. They found a gun that apparently belonged to the friend's older brother. The two of them were playing with it but didn't realise there was a bullet in the chamber. The gun went off and the bullet ricocheted off something and went straight into the boy's heart. He died. At just eighteen years old, and expecting his first baby with his girlfriend, my son was convicted of causing grievous bodily harm and sentenced to sixteen years' jail.

I was devastated and felt awful that I wasn't around to help him through this. I wrote him a letter, telling him to try to make the most of his time in prison. If he railed against it every day, it would kill him. If he tried to work with the system, at least when he came out he would be better prepared for life.

And then, miraculously, the day of my appeal arrived. The hearing didn't take long. The judge denounced my trial as a 'corrupt' process and ordered that I be immediately set free. My kids were all at court and cheered at the verdict, surrounding me with hugs and kisses.

I'd lost eighteen months, but I think I managed to come out a stronger, better person. I'd been a stolen child who'd just had more time stolen from me. But life was about to start anew.

Chapter Twenty-three
Rediscovering My Roots

When I got out of jail at the end of 1989, I was full of optimism for the future. I was free at last, and ready to shout it from the rooftops, but it took all my strength to keep up my courage.

Having David inside was a daily kick in the guts, and finding Kevin struggling, and still drinking, hit me hard, too. He'd lost track of his daughter Crystal and spent a lot of time searching for her. In addition, despite all the promises and congratulations, my job was no longer there, so I had to look for another. And Greg ... well, he'd got a new girlfriend in the interim and the pair were having a baby together, something he'd always wanted. It would have been easy to have gone back on the drink to keep my spirits up, so to speak, but I refused. I'd worked too hard in prison to throw all my progress away now.

I kept on looking for a job, visiting David and trying to help

Kevin get off the grog. I'd been to rehab a number of times and been clean before I'd gone to jail, and I used the lessons I'd learnt to give Kevin a supporting hand. The girls were doing well, and Philip was still with his girlfriend and having another child, so I knew they were all okay, which was a huge comfort. I concentrated on looking after Kevin, and also Cindy, who was still with the boyfriend I didn't much like. By now, I'd had so many hopeless men in my own life and, despite being only forty-three, I decided I was better off without them.

I got back in touch with my birth mother Esme and asked if we could catch up. She insisted on meeting me away from her house in an area of town where none of her family was likely ever to see us together. I'd grown tired of this routine by now. As we sat down in a café, I asked her straight out if she'd told her family about me yet, even though I felt like I already knew the answer.

'No, Dianne, I haven't,' she said, looking down into her cup.

I couldn't help feeling let down. 'But do you think you will?'

'Maybe one day.'

'But *when* one day?'

'I don't know. When the time's right.'

I sighed. 'Are you ashamed of me?' I asked bluntly.

'Of course not.'

'Then why not tell them? I'd really like to meet my half-sisters.'

'It's difficult,' she said. 'They might be upset to hear I had another child.'

'But what about me? How upset am I that you've never really acknowledged my existence? You've met all my family, but I've never been allowed to meet yours. I feel like you're hiding me in a cupboard and never want to let me out.'

We parted that day without our usual kiss and hug. For the first time, I started wondering if she'd ever introduce me to her daughters. I'd been the middle child, and maybe the one she'd rather forget.

*

About a year later, in July 1991, I was contacted by someone who said he was a cousin of mine. He wanted to let me know that one of my aunties from my Aboriginal family had died, and the funeral was being held where she'd lived in Cummeragunja. He invited me to come along. Cummeragunja was on a bend in the Murray near the Victorian town of Barmah, about 700 kilometres away from Corrimal, but I readily agreed.

There'd been a lot in the newspapers about Aboriginal affairs of late, with the Royal Commission into Aboriginal Deaths in Custody presenting its report that year, and I was becoming really interested. The Commission had unearthed a scandal. It found that many of the Aboriginal prisoners who'd died in custody might have survived had the authorities not been negligent, uncaring, or had followed procedures adequately. Others should never have been in custody at all. There were simply far too many Aboriginal people being locked up for comparatively minor offences.

I looked forward to learning more, and Cummeragunja seemed like the place to do it. It was, I'd found out, where many of my Yorta Yorta people lived. In the old days, their nation occupied an area of around 200,000 square kilometres in central Victoria, stretching from the Murray past Echuca in the west to the edge of the Victorian alps in the east, encompassing the waters of the Murray, Campaspe, Edwards and Goulburn rivers and Broken Creek – the river country. When the British arrived, settlers forced the Yorta Yorta off their traditional lands, killing them or herding them into 'reserves' run by the government or churches known as 'missions'. My ancestor William Cooper and his family ended up on a Christian mission called Maloga. This is where he began his political life, as one of the organisers of the Maloga Petition. As a result, two years later in 1883, land about 6 kilometres upriver was put aside to create the Cummeragunja Reserve. Five years later, most of the residents of Maloga moved there in protest against the strict religious rules of the old reserve, taking some of the buildings with them.

At first, things were good. The Aboriginal residents ran Cummera, as it was fondly known, as a farm, producing wool, wheat and dairy products, and were well on the way to self-sufficiency. But then *The Aborigines Protection Act 1909* – a terrible misnomer if ever there was one – abolished the local farmers' committee, and the NSW Board for the Protection of Aborigines assumed control. They took all the funds from the farm, doled out miserly rations in return, neglected housing and living conditions, removed children from their families and mostly trained the girls to be domestic servants for white families. The poor sanitation, food and water led to illnesses like TB and whooping cough, and the station manager ruled Cummera brutally, as if it were his own personal fiefdom, completely ignoring its proud, independent past and trying to crush the spirit of the educated and articulate people who lived there.

In 1939, the situation grew so bad and the residents so desperate that, at great risk to themselves, around 200 walked off the mission in protest, swimming the river to relocate to camps along the riverbank in Victoria. There they stayed through one of the most bitter winters on record, refusing to return. This became known throughout Australia as the 'Cummeragunja Walk-Off', the first mass strike of Indigenous people. It was a milestone in the struggle for Aboriginal rights and a symbol ever more of courage and fighting for justice in the face of almost impossible odds. It's a trek that has been commemorated every year since.

The rebels refused to give in and ultimately the government was forced into an about-turn. The station manager was moved off, but parcels of land after World War II were handed to white Australian returned servicemen and, needless to say, returned Indigenous servicemen were not eligible. Finally, in 1984, ownership of the land was passed to the newly created Yorta Yorta Local Aboriginal Land Council.

I was curious to see what the place was like and hopefully meet a few of my relatives. I'd asked Esme about it, but she'd said it was just an old graveyard and there wasn't really anything there. So when I arrived and found a teeming town with around 300 inhabitants, many of whom looked like Kevin, I was overwhelmed. Everyone was so welcoming, it made my heart sing. At last, I felt I was home among my family – my mother's people, the people of the river country. Apart from looking like Kevin, I could also see myself and the rest of my kids in them. They were friendly and outgoing and had many of the same values as I do. And they embraced me as a daughter of the river country. I fell instantly in love.

I stayed the night and met a few more members of my extended family. Uncle Alf 'Boydie' Turner was one of William Cooper's grandsons and a first cousin of my birth mother. He said he'd known of my birth but then no one knew what had happened to me. When I told him, and the others, parts of my story, I could see they were touched, and shook their heads in sadness. Many of them had similar stories of being stolen from their natural parents and ending up with very difficult lives as a result. I was lucky I had an adoptive mum who cared deeply for me, but when she died, everything fell apart. An adoptive dad who hates his child can do incredible damage.

But I loved the spirit of Cummera. The locals told me more of its proud history. The Cummeragunja Invincibles, for instance, were a Yorta Yorta Australian Rules football team that started up soon after the founding of the reserve in 1888. A lot of the neighbouring leagues wouldn't admit them, but finally they got into the Nathalia District Football Association and were undefeated through the 1898 and 1899 seasons. They ended up playing exhibition matches all over Victoria. The men of Cummera were later recognised as some of the best runners in Australia. One of William Cooper's sons, Lynch, won the top running race in the country, the Stawell Gift, in 1928 and became the first Indigenous Australian to win a world sporting title in the World Professional Sprint Championship in Melbourne the following year. Even today you can see the legacy of the Cummera sprinters, they told me, in the crouch start they were the first to champion, now used worldwide.

There were a host of well-known people who'd started out in Cummera as well. I'd had no idea. They reeled off their names like a real honour roll. Australian Rules footballer Douglas Nicholls, who was also a pastor and later governor of South Australia; Jack Charles, the actor and co-founder of Australia's first Indigenous theatre group; Jack Patten, founder of the Day of Mourning in NSW in 1938; opera singer Deborah Cheetham, whose grandparents took part in the Walk-Off and who was stolen from her mother when she was three weeks old and ... performer Jimmy Little. Jimmy Little! Suddenly, it clicked as to why I'd always felt such a bond with him. We went through the family lines and I was amazed and delighted at the end of it to discover he was my cousin. I couldn't wait to see him again and greet him as family.

I went back many, many times. For a year, I drove regularly from Corrimal to Cummera to see everyone. With not much work around home, I also started looking for jobs closer so visits would be easier. It was important to me to both get to know my family, and also learn more about my Aboriginal heritage and my culture. I really wanted to embrace that side of me.

I was walking with Uncle Boydie one day when a flock of magpies fluttered down near us. He expressed surprise that he'd never seen them there before. I told him they always seemed to turn up wherever I was and he smiled. 'Ah, I see,' he said. 'The magpie must be your totem.'

I read too about Eddie Mabo and his great fight to discredit the legal doctrine of 'terra nullius' – the idea that there was no one in this great land of Australia before the Europeans arrived, so they were free to claim it. I mourned along with my family when he died of cancer in January 1992 at the age of just fifty-five. But I celebrated with them when, on 3 June that year, the High Court announced its landmark Mabo decision, overturning the notion of terra nullius once and for all and officially recognising the Aboriginal inhabitants as the First Peoples.

I discussed it with Esme, but she didn't seem too interested. I was seeing her regularly, but still making little headway in persuading her to let me meet my half-sisters. I took her out for so many lunches and dinners, I started wondering if she perhaps saw me as a soft touch. She loved knitting and I'd buy her bags of wool. She'd then regale me with tales of which of her grandchildren she'd knitted clothes for, until I reminded her quite sharply one day that she had twelve great-grandchildren from me that she might think about knitting clothes for too. But she never did.

*

In March 1993, I was offered a job in Shepparton, on the Victorian side of the Murray River, 70 kilometres south of Cummera, as a youth worker with the Rumba Aboriginal Medical Service. I accepted eagerly and found a three-bedroom house to rent in Mooroopna for me, Cindy and Kevin. Cindy had just discovered she was pregnant, but I still didn't like her boyfriend, and Kevin was still drinking. I thought this could be the break with the past all three of us needed.

Kevin decided, however, that he didn't want to move to Mooroopna with Cindy and me. He was twenty-seven and naturally wanted to be more independent, so I left him in Corrimal with the promise that there would always be a bedroom reserved for him in Mooroopna if ever he changed his mind. He seemed fine with that and said he might come down later. Cindy's pregnancy was going well, and she was more settled now she was away from the boyfriend I didn't like. And I found I loved my new job. In fact, I was so enthusiastic, I took on more hours at the weekends as a worker for Juvenile Justice. I was in my element. The police would pick up young Koori kids, ring me and I'd go to the police station to check they were okay, and then sit with them in interviews, liaise with other agencies, talk to their families, attend any later court hearings and visit them if they were sent to rehab or to jail. I was on call twenty-four hours a day, but I didn't mind. It felt great to be helping people again.

One night, in September 1993, Kevin rang, sounding despondent and lonely.

'I just haven't been able to find Crystal,' he said. 'I miss her so much. And I'm missing you, Mum.'

'We miss you too, love,' I told him. 'Why don't you come down for a visit? You're always saying you will; how about now?'

'But I've got a couple of people staying at the house,' he said. 'I'm worried about the computer and all our stuff. I don't know that I should leave everything here.'

'Forget those,' I told him. 'Just get a good night's sleep and come down first thing in the morning. I've got your room all ready for you like I've always said.'

'Thanks, Mum. Yeah, I think I'll come.'

'Great. Now get some sleep. Love ya!'

Later that evening, he rang again to say he was still making up his mind. Then he rang again. I started getting worried. The fourth time the phone rang, I jumped on it. It was Debbie.

'I've just had an odd conversation with Kevin,' she said. 'He says he's thinking of coming down to stay with you in Victoria, but he can't make up his mind.'

I laughed. 'Yep, I've had the same conversation with him. Hopefully he'll decide to come tomorrow.'

Kevin rang twice more, and the last time he said he was going to watch some TV with a neighbour. 'That's a good idea,' I said. 'It's nice to have some company.'

'Yes, Mum,' he replied. 'It'll be fine. I'll call you in the morning.'

The next morning, the phone rang, and I answered it thinking it'd be Kevin. It wasn't. It was Linda.

'Oh, Mum,' she said in such a broken voice, I was instantly on high alert.

'What is it? Linda! What's wrong?'

'It's Kevin,' she said. 'Oh, Mum . . .'

There was a pause that felt like a lifetime and I knew I was holding my breath.

'Kevin . . . Kevin . . . he's gone and hanged himself.'

I dropped the phone, snatched up my car keys, made straight for the door and, before I even knew it, found myself on the road, driving straight to Wollongong Hospital. The rain was pouring down and I was crying so hard, I could barely see the road ahead.

But that made no difference. I drove like a woman possessed, with my foot down hard on the accelerator, always just above the speed limit, overtaking trucks, taking stupid chances, desperate to get there as quickly as I could. I had to see my son and make sure he was going to be all right. Why would he have done something like this? Why couldn't he have gone to bed and just driven down to see us the next day? What was happening with him?

I screeched to a halt outside the hospital and raced inside.

'I want to see my son,' I gasped to the receptionist. 'His name's Kevin O'Brien. He came in last night or this morning. Please, where can I find him?'

The woman went through a list on her desk and then looked up at me. 'Just wait here a moment. I think there's some of your family here. I'll get one of them to come down.'

'No, no,' I yelled. 'I don't want to see my family. I want to see my son. Kevin O'Brien. Which ward is he in?'

'Just a moment, Mrs O'Brien,' she said, and picked up the phone.

A moment later, a doctor in a white coat approached.

He put his hand on my arm. 'I'm sorry, Mrs O'Brien,' he said. 'They brought in your son last night. There was nothing we could do …'

At that moment, I realised Kevin must be dead, and all the fight left me. My knees buckled and the doctor helped me into a chair. 'Would you like to see him?' he asked softly.

I nodded, unable to speak.

Chapter Twenty-four
Living on River Country

It took a long, long time to come to terms with Kevin's death. I just couldn't believe that my first-born son was gone. There were moments when I'd forget he was dead, and I'd think to myself, 'I must tell Kevin that', or 'Kevin will laugh when he hears about this', and then reality would hit me like a ten-tonne truck and leave a searing pain in my chest. It hurt so badly at times, I didn't think I'd be able to bear it. But I knew I had to, if not for me, then for the sake of my other kids who were all in pain too, and Cindy, whose baby was due soon.

I don't remember much now about the hours and days that immediately followed. I didn't want to stay in our house in Corrimal as I didn't want to be where Kevin had killed himself. I blamed myself. I should have known how depressed he must have been. I should have helped him more in his search for Crystal. I should

226

never have gone to Victoria without him. I should have insisted he come down to join Cindy and me.

His funeral was beautiful and there were a lot of people who came to say goodbye: all our family; Kevin's friends; the elders from Shepparton; our aunties and uncles from Cummeragunja; and even my birth mother Esme, which I was happy about. I didn't bother to tell either Kevin's dad, Michael Brown, or my adoptive dad. They hadn't cared much about Kevin in life, so I sure as hell wasn't going to let them look as if they cared enough to come in death.

Cindy and I finally returned to Mooroopna with heavy hearts. We missed Kevin, we told each other every single day, and every night I struggled to get away from the pursuing shark. I tried to bury myself in my work, but some of the joy had gone out of it.

Out of the blue, a woman from Barmah, close to Cummera, called by our house and asked if I'd like to work at the old mission as an Aboriginal – Koori – health worker. I loved my regular visits there, so I eagerly agreed. It was an easy 70 kilometre drive and it would give me the chance to learn even more about my culture, while helping out the locals, many of whom were related to me. It was the perfect fit. I could help people, I could use my training as a youth worker and I could call on my own experience of abusing drink and drugs to advise people, knowledgeably, about how they could help themselves and lead healthier lifestyles.

The day I started my new job at the Cummeragunja Housing and Development Aboriginal Corporation (CHADAC) I remember being so happy. As a health worker, my varied role included everything from planning community development and health to putting in submissions, initiating projects with local government, doing the bookkeeping and banking and setting up partnerships with other agencies. I'd be given more responsibility as I got used to the way things were done there, and I was eager to do as much as I could.

Cindy gave birth on 25 November 1993 to a beautiful, healthy girl she decided to call Jedda. The 1950s movie of the same name had long been a favourite of ours, and even more since we'd discovered our Aboriginal heritage. It was the first movie to star two Aboriginal actors in leading roles, as well as – fittingly – the first Australian film to be shot in colour. About an Aboriginal girl called Jedda taken by a white woman to raise as her own, but who longs to discover her own culture, it appealed to me for obvious reasons. Debbie, Linda and Philip came to visit to meet Jedda, and we sent some photos to David in prison. He seemed to be doing all right. In his letters, he said he'd found Jesus and that was proving a huge comfort. The photos of baby Jedda stirred something else in me too, the memory of another baby, Kevin's little girl, Crystal. She'd be seven by now, I realised, and I decided I'd carry on Kevin's quest to find her and make sure she knew her family. Shortly after, Linda and her husband packed up their home and decided to come and live with us for good.

It was great to have my two girls and my granddaughter around me, but the house at Mooroopna was expensive and I was getting more and more tired driving so often between home and work. So when one of my uncles, an elder from Cummera, visited and said he was being allocated a house at the old mission by the Aboriginal Land Council and offered it to us, I was overjoyed. It was like a dream, the prospect of working where my people were originally from and living on my traditional river country, too. The day we all moved up there felt like the ultimate homecoming, with everyone at Cummera embracing me as the great-grandchild of William Cooper and welcoming us all with huge smiles and hugs.

Kevin, I felt with a pang, would have loved it.

*

I worked hard at Cummera and had some big wins. I divided my time between CHADAC and the Viney Morgan Clinic and seemed to be reinvigorating both. At the clinic, I started as an Aboriginal health worker and was given the freedom to spread my wings out over nearly every health issue we encountered. I learnt hearing health skills and was able to assess people who might need hearing aids; I was educated in diabetes and asthma and could offer advice to anyone suffering from them; and I ran a needle syringe exchange program to ensure that, if we had any drug users in the community, at least they'd have access to new needles and could be referred for help. I instigated a number of community health plans, projects and planning days, as well as assisting our doctors and putting in place HIV/AIDS education.

At the time, there was a fresh focus on Aboriginal health. Life expectancy for Aboriginal and Torres Strait Islander people was still about twenty years less than for other Australians. Aboriginal men tended to live only to the age of 59.4, as compared to other Australian males' 76.6 years, and our women till 64.8 against non-Aboriginal Australian women's 82 years. In addition, we suffered from more disease, and more acutely, too. Circulatory system disease, including heart disease and stroke, was the leading cause of death for Indigenous men and women, and our men were dying at 3.2 times the rate of men generally, and our women 2.8 times more than all Australian women.

The year 1993 was the International Year of the World's Indigenous Peoples and Paul Keating was prime minister and seemed to be taking the problems seriously. A Week of Prayer for Reconciliation began at the same time, supported by all the major religions in Australia. An Aboriginal man by the name of Charlie Perkins was more and more in the limelight – the very same man I'd so admired thirty years before in Walgett when he was leading the Freedom Riders. Now Dr Charles Perkins, he'd become a respected voice on Aboriginal affairs. He opened Australia's first National/ International Indigenous and Economic Conference in Alice Springs with a rousing speech. 'Unless the approaches to Aboriginal health are broadened,' he declared, 'to include greater attention to the health problems of adults, and are matched by broad-ranging strategies aimed at redressing Aboriginal social and economic disadvantages, it is likely that overall mortality will remain high.' I couldn't have agreed more.

There was so much to be done, and I threw myself into the task with enthusiasm. That first year, I managed to attract no less than $300,000 in grants into the village from all the submissions and applications I'd written. I also tried to boost pride in the place, with pictures of William Cooper on display, as well as the community feel, with family days and BBQs. I was eager to introduce my family to everyone living there as this was the extended family they'd never before had. Linda got involved too, and I invested $6000 of my own money in a house that nobody else wanted which Debbie's husband, a builder, renovated as a refuge for kids whose parents were drinking. We set up the community's first youth centre to give kids another place to go and things to do and the old mission school was turned into a museum. Soon Debbie came and joined us and gave us all a helping hand.

Esme visited but we seemed to have hit a roadblock in our relationship. The fact that she was keeping me from meeting my half-sisters – my only real family apart from my own kids and her – still rankled. But however much I pleaded with her, she'd always avoid the subject. As a result, I could feel the anger building up in me each time we met. Even worse, she offered me little titbits about her life that I think she thought would satisfy me, but they had the opposite effect. They just made me feel more frustrated.

'You know, I really loved your father,' she told me one time as I was driving her to the station for her trip back to Sydney. 'I was going out with him and thought he was wonderful. But when I fell pregnant and he turned out to have made another girl pregnant and was going to marry her ... I was devastated.'

'Yes, that's terrible,' I said, trying to sound sympathetic, although, in fact, I was just hungry for more information. 'Did you ever see him again?'

'Yes, I'd keep bumping into him and he was friends of friends of mine, so I always knew where he was.'

'That's until he had the heart attack and died?' I asked gently.

An odd expression came on her face which I couldn't quite fathom. 'Yes, that's right, Dianne. Until he died.'

'What was his name?' I asked.

'Steve.'

'And his surname?'

'That doesn't matter now.'

'But it does to me,' I said, trying not to sound too whiny, as I pulled up outside the train station.

'Well, he's gone now. So it doesn't make any difference.'

And with that, she opened the car door and was gone again.

*

In 1994, the chairperson of CHADAC had to go away for six months and I was asked to fill his position. My responsibilities grew hugely. I helped coordinate infrastructure projects, like schemes to provide clean drinking water and upgrades to the sewerage system, and set up projects such as a screen-printing workshop and a sewing workshop. My daughters were amazed that I seemed to be able to turn my hand to anything but, as I told them, if you're determined enough, you can achieve almost everything. I was always keen to be a role model for my daughters and the other younger women in the community. I also took on more projects in women's health and justice and became the housing and rent officer for the organisation. I drew up community business plans, forged more partnerships with local councils and other agencies, and worked with the Victorian Department of Education and Early Childhood Development and Centrelink to help people into further education or meaningful employment. I also became the CEO of the Aboriginal Medical Service in the community.

With such a rapid ascent, I was bound to encounter a few problems. Most people were grateful for the work I was doing to improve their lives, but a few were jealous and wanted me to fail. I made a powerful enemy of one influential person in the community but, after a while, just tried to ignore his attempts to undermine me. In any small community or village, there are going to be rifts and people who don't get on, but I kept my head down and pushed forward. Because I was a non-drinker, people were always asking me to give them lifts to Echuca, about 30 kilometres south-west on the other side of the river. Eventually, I grew tired of it. After three years, Linda and her husband decided to leave and pick up their life again elsewhere. I missed them but was even busier, also serving on the executive of the Aboriginal Health and Medical Research Council's peak body back in Sydney.

In 1996, the Council for Aboriginal Reconciliation launched Australia's first National Reconciliation Week, which had grown out of that original Week of Prayer for Reconciliation three years earlier. The week of 27 May to 3 June each year would commemorate two milestones in the reconciliation journey: the successful 1967 referendum and the Mabo High Court decision. It was intended to be a time for all Australians to learn about Aboriginal history, cultures and achievements, and explore how they could each make a contribution to reconciliation, helping to create a stronger Australia as a result.

It was a period of enormous excitement and optimism, when it seemed black and white were finally coming together. But it was a long, and often painful, journey. My Yorta Yorta people, with our long-necked turtle totem, started putting together a native title claim over some of our traditional lands in northern Victoria, but it was turning into a long and harrowing battle. There was fresh focus too on the issue of the stolen generations – Aboriginal babies taken from their mothers and their families – and there were heart-rending stories in the press daily of the toll that official government policy had inflicted.

The following year, 1997, I was invited to a luncheon in Sydney hosted by then NSW Premier Bob Carr who was the first to make an official apology to us. The Aboriginal flag with its stirring image of a golden sun against black, representing the Aboriginal people of Australia, and red, as in the red earth and ochre used in Aboriginal ceremonies, was flown in the chamber. It was an overwhelming occasion as it brought back memories of my adoptive father being so cruel to me, and thoughts of what might had been, had I not been taken from my real mother.

Nearly all of us there were revisiting, and replaying, similar traumas.

I noticed one woman at the formal lunch was looking at me intently.

'Hello!' I said, cheerily. 'I'm sorry, do I know you?'

'You're Dianne, aren't you? I think my brother is going out with a friend of yours. His name's Danny.'

I thought back to my life in Sydney. 'Ah yes!' I said, remembering. 'He's with my friend Emma, I think.'

'Yes, that's right,' she said, beaming. 'I thought it was you. I haven't seen you for a long time, though. Are you still in Mount Druitt?'

'No,' I said, and told her all about Cummeragunja. She seemed fascinated and we chatted for a good ten minutes. At the end of it, however, she said she couldn't get over how much I looked like her cousin.

'Really?' I said. 'What's her name?'

'Her name's Jenny,' she said. 'Her mum's Esme.'

My heart lurched. I knew those names.

'She looks so much like you,' she continued. 'She's got four sisters. Lives in Helensburgh.'

I took a deep breath. 'I guess the reason she looks like me is because she's my half-sister.'

Chapter Twenty-five
The Dream of Five Sisters

Being told I looked so much like one of my half-sisters, Jenny, haunted me. I went back to Cummeragunja and tried to forget it by burying myself in work. I was busier than ever anyway, especially with the Federal Court dismissing the Yorta Yorta land claim in 1998, saying that they had ceased to occupy their traditional lands in accordance with traditional laws and customs before the end of the nineteenth century. The controversial finding crushed many people's spirits, and was received with horror by countless other Aboriginal groups.

The judge claimed that 'the tide of history has indeed washed away any real acknowledgement of their traditional laws and any real observance of their traditional customs'. It made people fear that perhaps only those native claims on land that had never been occupied by Europeans might succeed in future. Appeals against the ruling were immediately lodged.

Despite all the hullabaloo, I still couldn't forget the conversation I'd had with that woman at the reconciliation lunch. I longed to make contact with my half-sisters but, by 1999, I'd now known my birth mother for fifteen years and it seemed pretty unlikely she was ever going to introduce me to her daughters.

I decided to take matters into my own hands. What did I have to lose?

I now knew Jenny lived in Helensburgh, 45 kilometres south of Sydney, so one weekend I drove up from Cummera and tried to find her. I arrived, parked by the row of shops and then felt a bit silly. How do you look for someone you know so little about? I wondered what she did for a living and what kind of woman she might be. I got out of the car and looked around. Directly in front of me was a chemist. Perfect. Everyone goes to a chemist.

I walked in and smiled at the chemist on duty. 'I know this sounds a bit silly,' I said to him, 'but I'm looking for my half-sister, Jenny. I don't suppose you know any Jennys who live in town, do you?'

He looked at me. 'As a matter of fact, I do,' he said. 'She'd be maybe five years older than you.'

'Yes, that's right,' I said, suddenly excited. 'Can you tell me what she looks like?'

'That's easy,' he smiled. 'Just stand over here.'

I moved to where he was indicating but must have looked mystified.

'Now look straight ahead,' he instructed.

I looked ahead and saw a mirror and my own face reflected in it.

'You want to know what she looks like?' he asked. 'She looks just like that.'

He told me where to find her and, taking a deep breath, I drove straight there. I knocked on her door, she opened up and looked bewildered, then I told her who I was. He was right; there was no mistaking we were related.

'Wow!' she cried. 'Wow! Who would have known? But why didn't Mum tell us we had another sister?'

I shook my head. 'I honestly don't know. Maybe she was nervous about your reaction?'

'But I think it's great!' Jenny said. 'Wait till the others find out!'

We had a long chat and I warmed to her immediately. It was wonderful to have found more of my family and I was delighted when she said she'd be happy to introduce me to her sisters, Barbara, Geraldine, Patricia and Shirley.

'Welcome home, sis,' she said. 'It's great to find you.'

*

The next day, Esme called, none too pleased that I'd tracked Jenny down. But, I reasoned with her, she was never going to introduce me, so maybe it was better I did it myself. It was the start of the cooling of our relationship.

Back in Cummera, things were up and down. In 1999, I was appointed CEO of the Aboriginal Medical Service, and found I was doing pretty much everything, from managing doctors' appointments and pathologies to education programs on safe sex and asthma; from consulting on housing policies to running programs on – my speciality – domestic violence.

One day, I had a knock on my office door and who should walk in but Jimmy Little.

'Little Dianne!' he exclaimed when he saw me. 'What are you doing here?'

'I work here!' I said as we hugged each other. 'It's so great to see you.'

He leant back to get a better look at me. 'After all this time,' he said and laughed. 'And now it turns out we're related too. Fair dinkum, cuz!'

That year was a big one for Aboriginal Australia. The organisation Reconciliation Australia was launched and, in Sydney, around 300,000 people walked across the Harbour Bridge to show their support.

As for my own reconciliation, two of my other half-sisters, Barbara and Shirley, came to Cummera and were shocked to find so much going on, such a large population, and how important I was in the community. They said Esme had told them, as she had me, that it was nothing but an old graveyard. They were eager to learn about their Aboriginal side too, saying they knew little about their heritage. I was pleased to help, and it was great to get to know each other. Within months, they'd set up a meeting for me with all my half-sisters at our youngest sister's place in Liverpool in south-west Sydney. I was thrilled and grateful to finally get to know them, though my joy was tinged with sadness that they'd been living so close to us all this time and that my kids had missed out on growing up knowing their cousins. Even harder, perhaps Kevin might have still been alive today had he known he had close family nearby to call on in his hour of need.

Esme only came out to Cummera once more. She was still angry I'd had meetings with her daughters. Her husband, the father of two of my half-sisters, had died a few months earlier. She told me that he'd actually seen me with her, and used to laughingly refer to me as her 'lesbian friend' because he sometimes saw me dropping her off and we'd kiss goodbye. I smiled, but was secretly horrified that she'd let him think that. At about the same time, she told me my real father's surname was Hamilton. He'd been Steve Hamilton. She said he'd also recently died.

'But no ...' I said. 'You told me ages ago that he was already dead!'

'Well, Dianne, I wanted to protect you.'

'Protect me?' I echoed. 'Protect me from what?'

'I didn't know you very well then.'

'But what difference would that have made?'

'I thought I was doing it for the best,' she said lamely.

I had to leave the room at that point as I was so angry, I could hardly contain it. Ever since I'd found out I was adopted, I'd wanted to meet my birth father to expunge the memory of my adoptive father. And now she'd robbed me forever of that chance. I felt sick to my heart.

*

In April 2000, I felt it was time to leave Cummera. Saying goodbye to my family and friends was heart-rending, but I knew my time had come to an end there. I'd achieved so much, but it was right to pass on the baton to others.

I stayed for a while in Wollongong, south of Sydney, with one of my grandsons, then moved to Gosford on the Central Coast with my daughter Linda. My youngest daughter Cindy applied for a Housing Commission house nearby in Woy Woy, and managed to be allocated one, so we moved in there. It felt like the right decision the first time I walked along our street and all the neighbours expressed amazement that I was the only one not to be attacked by magpies. 'They're my totem,' I told them, as if that explained everything. I enrolled at the local TAFE and did more research on my family history. The more I learnt, the more I thought I should write a book about my heritage and my life.

Once planted, that thought never quite went away.

I found work with the local needle exchange program which provided clean injecting equipment to drug users and, at the same time, offered them education, support and referrals to rehabilitation programs. It was still very much an experiment at that stage, but has now been acclaimed as saving many lives. Users no longer had to inject secretly in dark alleyways, but came to clean clinics where they could be supervised and diverted to other programs. I looked after most of our Aboriginal clients. The following year, 2001, I applied for a part-time job in drug and alcohol health promotion and created a package for Koori women with alcohol problems. It was a big undertaking, which took all of ten months, and was called 'If You Want a Taste of the Spirits, Turn to Your Culture'. It was a huge success.

Off the back of that, I was offered a job in the Northern Sydney Central Coast Area Health Service's HIV/sexual health unit. It was a wonderful position. It enabled me to help people to my heart's content with their health issues, providing education, community development and clinical services.

'This,' I told my daughter Debbie one day, 'is what I think I was born to do. I've finally found my life's work after so long looking for it. I want to make my family proud of me.'

'Oh Mum!' she replied. 'We're already so proud of you. To get through all you've faced and still now be helping so many other people ... We couldn't have wished for a better mum or role model.'

I couldn't say anything, I was so full of emotion. We just hugged each other. Looking back, I think it was the start of a period of real healing from all the hurt of the past.

I still kept an eye on what was happening back at Cummera. Appeals against the dismissal of their native title claim trundled on but the last one, to the High Court of Australia, was finally dismissed on 12 December 2002 on a five-to-two majority ruling. It left so many people there absolutely heartbroken.

It was ironic that, at the same time, others were celebrating one of the heroes of the Yorta Yorta, my great-grandfather William Cooper, for his contribution to the world. A plaque was unveiled that year in the Jewish Holocaust Centre in Melbourne in honour of 'the Aboriginal people for their actions protesting against the persecution of Jews by the Nazi Government of Germany in 1938'.

I wondered what might have happened had they passed on his letter to the German consulate back then. At least the Jewish community recognised what good we'd tried to do.

Of course, there was never any shortage of drama in my own family. We'd been thrilled when my youngest son, David, had finally been released from prison after fourteen years; two years shy of his full term. We'd welcomed him home with a big party, and I was happy to see him refusing alcohol as he was still very religious. I felt sure he'd have the odd lapse, but he seemed determined to build a worthwhile life for himself after so long behind bars.

He certainly had that good Samaritan gene. One night in November 2003, in Saratoga on the Central Coast, he was woken by his girlfriend who told him a nearby house was on fire. He leapt up and rushed over to find smoke billowing from the home. Some neighbours were already there, saying there was no one inside, but David heard a faint scream and told everyone to be quiet. He heard it again and raced to the back of the house and saw a four-year-old girl through the window, flames already licking the floor around her. He didn't hesitate: he smashed the window with a table that stood outside, jumped through, picked up the girl and ran through the house to the locked front door, breaking it down with a surfboard to get them both out. He handed the child to a neighbour and then tried to go back again to see if anyone else was there, but was beaten back by the flames. He was hailed a hero by the local newspaper, and I was so proud of him.

Despite our best efforts, we weren't always successful in saving every child, though. Ever since Kevin's death ten years before, I'd been trying to track down his daughter Crystal. She was always on my mind, and I felt responsible for her with Kevin gone.

Finally, in 2003, I managed to trace her through Centrelink and I called her and invited her over to stay. When she arrived, instantly I could see in her Kevin's tortured soul. She was an unhappy eighteen-year-old, drinking too much and lacking direction, and she told me she'd suffered a number of mental health problems. She said she missed her dad dreadfully and had sometimes fallen so deeply into depression that, starting at the age of thirteen, she'd made a number of attempts on her own life. I talked to her about Kevin and how much he'd missed her and gave her some more photos of him. I was touched when she had them printed onto pillowcases so she could always sleep with her head on his shoulder. Crystal ended up living with us for six months but eventually moved out. We saw her only sporadically after that. In 2009 we received the terrible news that she was dead. She'd apparently been in a mental health facility but escaped and walked onto the train tracks at Albion Park in Shellharbour and into the path of an oncoming train.

I was, again, heartbroken. We buried her in a snow-white coffin and put a wooden cross and purple flowers on the fence near where she died. The only thought that provided any small scrap of comfort was that she was now, once more, back in the arms of her dad.

*

The past has a habit of returning. In 2003, us former inmates of Parramatta Girls Home got together for the first time. ABC TV covered the reunion in a series of broadcasts on the 'Stateline' program. Listening to the other women talking about their experiences brought the horror of it all back again. We discussed making a joint claim for compensation from the NSW government that had so clearly been negligent in the way they'd treated us but, in the end, discussions broke down. It was so hard, I think, to reach consensus as we'd all been damaged in different ways. We agreed to make individual claims instead, but I knew that was going to be difficult. I applied, for instance, for my files from the home, but when I saw them, nearly everything had been redacted. How can you possibly fight for justice in those circumstances?

I also had a call from Uncle Ken. He said he'd been trying to catch me for weeks. He had some news he didn't know if I'd be happy to hear or not.

'Well, tell me what it is, and we'll both know,' I said.

'Your dad ... he's dead,' he said bluntly. 'He was in a home and we think he had a heart attack.'

In truth, I felt neither happy nor sad. I just felt empty. With Ronnie God knows where – I hadn't heard from him in years and suspected he might even be dead too – that was my last direct link with Mum. But I certainly didn't shed a tear for him.

Instead, I decided to look forward and get on with the rest of my life. I found out my birth dad, Steve Hamilton, who was also Aboriginal, had later had a son and a daughter and, while my half-brother didn't want to see me, I met my half-sister and we established a real bond. I'd also been shown some pictures of my dad, and loved looking at them and imagining what might have been. I had a lot of other relatives too on that side of the family and hoped that one day we could all meet up in one big family reunion. It hasn't yet happened, but I'm always hopeful.

Life, somehow, just kept getting in the way. One day, after finding a lump under my arm, I received a diagnosis of another cancer, this time non-Hodgkin lymphoma, but was told it was a type that was very slow to develop. While the doctors would keep an eye on me, I didn't need any treatment, which was good news. I was still loving my work with Central Coast Health, and Debbie was now following in my footsteps, working for the Aboriginal Medical Service in Wollongong, doing great work to improve the health of Aboriginal people. The rest of my family seemed settled too and, at fifty-nine, I now had twenty-four grandchildren from my kids, fourteen great-grandchildren and, most incredibly, five new sisters (six, if you counted the sister from my birth dad).

Chapter Twenty-six
Spirit Undaunted

When a reporter from *The Senior* newspaper called me in November 2005 and asked me for an interview, I didn't think anything of it. I sat down and talked about my life, and then got back to work. I forgot all about it until my phone started ringing off the hook. Friends and colleagues were congratulating me on the story. What story? I had no idea what they were on about until I went out to the newsagents in my break and saw the newspaper on the rack – with my photo on the front page. I stared at it, stunned. The caption read: 'From hardship to a source of inspiration.'

I opened the paper and saw myself again. 'Spirit undaunted', the headline said. 'The life of a remarkable woman who overcame incredible hardship and uncertainty to become an inspiration to her people.' And there was my story, from being a baby of the stolen generation to my life now. I was overcome with emotion. How amazing that people around the country would be reading about me! If only Mum were still alive, she would have been so proud. I sat down at my desk that afternoon and had a little cry.

But it was no time for self-congratulation. I was busy with my work at Central Coast Health and my responsibilities were stretching over a wider and wider area. I held Koori workshops with young people, did cultural awareness programs for non-Aboriginal people, trained other sexual health workers, advocated for people with HIV/AIDS and other blood-borne viruses, ran education projects for Hep C and – because having fun is an essential part of good health – organised a Koori sports day. I visited schools to talk about sexual health, promoted World AIDS Day, formed partnerships with other organisations and taught women's health, men's health and youth health and, at the other end of the spectrum, elders' health.

I was receiving great feedback for my work. Some wrote letters praising me for my professionalism, others for my dedication to improving people's self-esteem. 'She is knowledgeable and speaks with candour,' one of my bosses wrote. 'Dianne is respected by the community and ... is in an ideal position to provide leadership for our community. She is a proud Aboriginal woman and her example has non-Aboriginal people and organisations wanting to be a part of any program or action she involves herself in.' Although I'd had a tough life, it taught me so many lessons I could use to help other people. I never hesitated to talk about my own experiences if I thought it could work for others, too.

In 2006, I joined Mingaletta, an Aboriginal and Torres Strait Islander community hub based in Umina on the Woy Woy peninsula area of the Central Coast. Mingaletta started in 2002 providing a range of services, programs and activities in health, welfare, culture and education, all aimed at improving the quality of life for our people. It also offered youth and family support, especially to those who were homeless, displaced or at risk of family breakdown. We were volunteers, doing everything in our spare time, but it felt so worthwhile, it added an extra dimension to my life. By the end of that year, predictably enough, I'd become chairperson, and been nominated for a Gosford City Australia Day Community Award for outstanding service. I was also nominated for the Aboriginal and Torres Strait Islander Commission (ATSIC) Regional Council elections. In the end, I missed out by just one vote. I didn't mind too much. I felt I could do so much good outside the bureaucracy and that was enough for me.

*

I often talked to people about my experiences in Parramatta Girls Home, and in 2007 I was pleased that it became a topic of much wider public conversation. The reunions with girls who'd been there were continuing but the trauma was getting even more of a mainstream airing. Playwright Alana Valentine, who'd seen one of the *Stateline* TV programs in 2003, had been so moved, she wrote a play, *Parramatta Girls*, telling our story. It premiered at the prestigious Belvoir Street Theatre in Sydney in March 2007, directed by Wesley Enoch and with Leah Purcell in one of the lead roles. Later that year the script was published, painting a heartbreaking picture of women being brutalised, drugged, raped and confined in solitary. I like to think it brought our plight to the eyes of a whole new audience.

It also increased pressure on the Australian government to recognise how badly so many people – particularly Aboriginal people – had been treated in the past. With the reconciliation movement gaining traction, there seemed to be a national outpouring of grief on behalf of Indigenous Australians. It culminated on 13 February 2008 with the then prime minister Kevin Rudd presenting an apology to us as a motion to be voted on by the House. 'We apologise for the laws and policies of successive parliaments and governments that have inflicted profound grief, suffering and loss on these our fellow Australians,' he said. It was a wonderful moment, a recognition of our suffering. But sadly, it didn't change things much for many of us.

On 6 December 2008, my great-grandfather William Cooper was again in the news. It was the seventieth anniversary of his protest to the Nazi government about their treatment of Jewish people, and his grandson and my uncle, Uncle Boydie, was presented – in the Parliament of Victoria in front of an audience that included lots of Yorta Yorta people, the premier John Brumby and the federal Indigenous affairs minister Jenny Macklin – a certificate from the Israeli ambassador, who said seventy Australian trees were being planted in Israel to commemorate William Cooper.

I talked to Esme about it, but she was, by then, quite sick. She eventually died on 10 October 2009. I thought the tragedy might draw me and my sisters closer, but sadly it had the opposite effect. I was upset that Esme's estate was divided among my five half-sisters but I was given only a fraction of what they received. It felt like a slap in the face for me and my kids and grandkids and great-grandkids that we were somehow 'less' related to her, and less deserving, than her other children and grandkids. Hopefully one day we'll get over that hurt and become a tighter family.

Meanwhile, William Cooper's star continued to rise. In October 2010, a court complex was opened in Melbourne called the William Cooper Justice Centre, and in December of that year, another of his great-grandchildren, Kevin Russell, re-enacted the walk from his home to meet up with Uncle Boydie in Federation Square in the centre of Melbourne. In addition, in Israel, an academic chair was created in his honour to support resistance in World Holocaust Studies, a tribute was held at Yad Vashem World Holocaust Remembrance Center, and the Australia Israel Leadership Forum hosted an associated Gala Dinner attended by Kevin Rudd, Julie Bishop and Israeli prime minister Benjamin Netanyahu. I felt so proud, all over again.

Locally, our efforts were being rewarded, too. I'd put in a submission that our Mingaletta organisation was growing so big, we needed our own premises. In 2010, we moved from the back of the local library into a former scout hall that had been damaged by fire. It was a fine building not far from the beach and it allowed us to do so much more with our limited resources. I get such a kick out of helping someone who comes here and might not have a home, or might be driving an unregistered car, who might have lost their job and have a fine they can't afford to pay. They walk out, and we've done our best to house them, pay their fine, organise for them to get their car registered and sometimes even found them a job. I'm incredibly proud of the work we do.

Aboriginal pride nationally was growing all the time, not least for us Yorta Yorta people. In 2012, the movie *The Sapphires* was released to enormous acclaim. It told the story of four young Aboriginal singers in the 1960s who form an all-girl singing group and end up entertaining the troops in Vietnam. It was based on a play which was, in turn, loosely based on real life. The four girls – Naomi Mayers, Beverly Briggs, Laurel Robinson and Lois Peeler – were all Yorta Yorta, from Cummeragunja, with mothers who'd been part of the famous Cummeragunja Walk-Off. They were played by some of the most wonderful young actors in Australia: Deborah Mailman, Jessica Mauboy, Shari Sebbens and Miranda Tapsell, with Irish actor and comedian Chris O'Dowd playing their drunken manager. It was a fabulously uplifting movie and made its world premiere at the 2012 Cannes Film Festival in May and then opened in Australia in August and in the US in 2013.

Fittingly, in 2012, William Cooper's grandson Uncle Alf led a re-enactment of the 1938 march from Footscray to the German consulate and, this time, the German consul general finally accepted a copy of his grandfather's protest letter. For sports fans, the William Cooper Cup became the annual trophy awarded to the winner of an Australian Rules football match between the Aboriginal All-Stars and Victoria Police. It was an excellent tribute to a man who, in life, had been relentlessly harassed, but was now recognised as an exceptional human being. Later came still more, including the Australian Electoral Commission renaming the Federal seat of

'Batman' after John Batman, one of the founders of the city of Melbourne, to 'Cooper' in his honour, with plans for a huge march in 2019 retracing his steps of the Walk-Off to mark its eightieth anniversary.

Everything was going so well, I could hardly believe it. I had applied for a Housing Commission home and that came through too, a magnificent four-bedroom house in Blue Haven, 55 kilometres north of Umina. It was perfect, and Cindy's daughter Jedda, her children and I all moved in, as well as a bunch of magpies who took up residence in the trees nearby. I saw it as a good sign.

And then the unthinkable happened. Late one evening in March 2013 we got a phone call from the police. There'd been an accident. Could I come to the hospital? It was my first-born, Debbie.

While working in Wollongong, Debbie had been living in Nowra on the south coast of NSW, an hour's drive away. That evening after work she'd gone to pick up her youngest grandchild, and had strapped the two-year-old girl into the child's seat behind her. In the pouring rain, her car had hit a deep puddle and had careened out of control, across the median strip and into the path of an oncoming vehicle. Debbie was killed instantly. The local pastor she'd been friendly with rushed to the scene of the accident to give her the last rites. Her granddaughter, thank God for small mercies, was untouched.

My whole family was stunned. Gorgeous, sweet Debbie, who'd never said a bad word about anybody, who'd never done a thing wrong in her life, who was helping so many people in her work and who'd never had a living enemy, was gone. I felt hollow all over again, with the same pain as when I'd lost Mum and Kevin and Crystal. I knew, however, that I had to stay strong, for her brothers and sisters, her kids and grandkids. We were all hurting, but I'd been through it before and I knew that somehow we'd come out the other side.

Over 1000 people attended Debbie's funeral. There was a tremendous outpouring of love for the little girl I'd lived for, and the beautiful woman at fifty years old she'd become. I'd hoped she would carry on my work after I was gone, but now that would never be.

Chapter Twenty-seven
Because of Her, We Can

As it had before, and always does, life carried on. A barrier was erected in the middle of the road where Debbie had died to hopefully prevent accidents like that in the future. I changed jobs in 2014, moving into general practice, becoming an Aboriginal outreach worker, and then the Aboriginal health manager. As always, I poured myself into my work.

Increasingly, as I'd moved up the previous organisation, I'd found myself more office-bound, working on the computer devising strategies and overseeing policy. Now I relished being back with other people, helping them as best I could, and seeing them respond. I became the manager of Mingaletta, too, and made sure we offered help to anyone who walked in our door – whether they were Aboriginal or not.

Maryanne, for instance, was an Indigenous woman who'd been

a victim of domestic violence and had run away from her husband. She was sleeping down at the beach and had no food, nowhere to live, no paperwork or ID and no clean clothes. I had a soft spot for women like her, having been in exactly the same position so many times throughout my own life. I rang the courts to organise for an Apprehended Violence Order against Maryanne's husband, so he wouldn't be able to come near her again, and then called the Housing Commission and all the housing co-ops who offered emergency accommodation to see if we could find her a new home. In the meantime, I gave her a tent to sleep in at the beach and a blow-up mattress. When, after a day or so, we still hadn't found her anywhere decent to stay, I called our MP and the opposition and asked them to put pressure on the department. She had a place to stay within the week.

Then I called the Salvation Army and St Vincent de Paul to get her some furniture, and did the rounds of supporters and donors we knew to find her clothes and a supply of food. Often, if we couldn't get enough, we'd raid our own cupboards at home and donate money from our own pockets too. And then I offered her some counselling. Like so many women in that position – including me in the past – Maryanne was in a torment of indecision. Maybe it had been her fault he struck out, she said. Maybe she'd done something wrong. Maybe if she was a better person, he'd change. I listened and then talked about my own story. She had done nothing wrong, I told her; there is simply no good reason on earth for a man to hit a woman. And he won't change. Get out while you can. These days, we told her, there's plenty of help at hand for women fleeing domestic violence, the police take it seriously, and we'd make sure she was okay. Sure enough, today she is.

Another day, a non-Indigenous man called Pete stopped by. He was an alcoholic and had just lost his job, had no food and was on the verge of losing his house, too. He was in desperate need of help. I referred him to the services who could give him a hand and, while he was waiting, gave him some work to do – mowing the lawns and clearing up the yard, for which I paid him $50. It was much better than a handout, as work enables people to keep their pride. He made a great job of it and we managed to find him more casual work. Today, he's four years sober and doing really well.

Later on, we conducted a survey about Mingaletta's services, asking the people we'd seen over the years the question: What would you have done if Mingaletta wasn't here? Sixty-three Aboriginal women said they would have died. That shocked me to the core. One woman said she'd been drinking at home, never saw anyone and was lonely and desperate until a white neighbour came to us saying she was concerned. We went to see the woman, brought her in to be part of our women's group so she could listen to us yarning and have a chat herself. It changed her life, she said. The neighbour later came by and thanked us, saying the woman was so much happier, was off the grog, eating healthy food and exercising regularly.

We like to think we never sent anyone away unhappy with the service we provided. Strangely enough, around that time I finally stopped having those nightmares about being chased by sharks that had haunted me nearly all my life. Maybe I finally felt in control of my own destiny.

*

I never asked for thanks, but suddenly I seemed to be receiving plenty. In federal parliament in 2014 I was named as one of three finalists in the NSW/ACT Regional Achievement and Community Awards for my 'outstanding' achievements and contribution. Chris Holstein, the MP for Gosford, made a touching speech. 'Di is a very special individual,' he said. 'She was selected because of her guidance, encouragement and much-needed support within her community. Dianne, or Aunty Di as we know her, has worked passionately for her community to assist in furthering the health and wellbeing of Aboriginal people – something she continues to do as an Aboriginal health manager at Medicare Local and as the volunteer chairperson for the Mingaletta community group.'

I didn't win, but it was lovely to be recognised.

In 2017 came the biggest surprise, however. On Sunday 29 October – Grandparents' Day – I was announced as the winner of the title of NSW Grandmother of the Year. I was completely taken aback. I was seventy-one years old by then, and had, sadly, only four of my six children still alive, but I had thirty-four grandchildren and a stunning fifty-six great-grandchildren. The citation said that 'Aunty Di has helped raise four generations of her own family'. I guess that was true.

I lost my mum when I was just fourteen, and I wanted to make sure I was always there for my children. I loved my kids, and I loved their kids ... and now their kids, too. I was thrilled when one of my great-granddaughters started showing an interest in her Aboriginal heritage and wanted to play an active role in her culture. But I still had plenty of room in my heart for any other kids who needed my help. I offered them that in my job in the practice, and personally, sponsoring children in need from Bangladesh through World Vision. Kids are kids, no matter where they're from. But still, I was shocked to be named Grandmother of the Year, but so very proud. The minister for ageing, Tanya Davies, even praised me, saying I'd won because of my 'selfless determination to improve the lives of countless children'. I suppose she was right.

It was a funny day, though. As she presented me the award, I mentioned that it had been nice to enter through the front door of the NSW Parliament House this time. When she asked what I meant, I confessed that, thirty-four years before, I'd actually climbed up the side of the building on some scaffolding and broken in! I smuggled in an Aboriginal flag that a few of us were planning to unfurl behind Pat O'Shane. Pat was going to be inducted as the first Aboriginal magistrate in NSW.

Unfortunately, I was the only one to make it into the building. I positioned the flag in the chamber ready for the big moment, but instead of regally opening, it just dropped to the ground.

I never had much luck with flags in my activist career. During the 1988 Bicentenary of the First Fleet's arrival, a group of us staged a protest in Sydney. One of my jobs was to stand in the water off Mrs Macquarie's Chair with two other activists, a married couple, and hold up a massive Aboriginal flag. I was in the middle, with the husband and wife at either end. As the flag got wetter, it became more and more heavy. Then a whitefella in a motorboat roared up and started throwing cans at us. The husband immediately dropped his end and went to shield his wife, but the flag was just too heavy for me to keep holding up on my own. I was also terrified of sharks in the harbour. It wasn't my proudest moment.

But there's been plenty to celebrate since. In 2014, I received an Australian Award for forty years of community service, and in 2016, Senator Deborah O'Neill put me forward for a Central Coast Women's Leadership Award as an Aboriginal woman 'reshaping the world for a more equal future'.

Then, in 2018, came another great honour. As chairperson of Mingaletta, I was selected to have my image projected onto the magnificent Central Station Clock Tower in Surry Hills. Built in 1921, it's Sydney's tallest clock tower and rises up 85 metres over Australia's busiest train station to look out over the whole of the city. It's one of our best-known landmarks and heritage icons. They beamed a giant version of me, along with a few other women, from 6 p.m. to midnight during NAIDOC Week. The theme was one of celebrating the invaluable contribution of Aboriginal and Torres Strait Islander women in communities, families, history and the nation, with the maxim, 'Because of her, we can!'

I could hardly believe I'd been chosen, but the NSW Trains service's Mark Champley said I was projected up there to 'acknowledge [my] resilience, hard work and commitment to the community'. He went on to say, 'Aunty Di has been the chairperson of Mingaletta for almost ten years and an active community volunteer for over forty ... [It's] a story of a woman who has inspired others within community and country because of her actions.'

I was enormously touched and honoured, and I loved travelling down to Sydney at night with all my family to stare up at myself ... and if that sounds weird, that's because it was. Even stranger, I could swear I saw a lone magpie flying past even though it's rare they come out at night. As I looked up and saw my giant self gazing towards the horizon, I couldn't help marvelling at how far I'd come, from a little girl lost to a woman the whole of Sydney was now – like it or not – having to look up to.

To top that off, we also produced a two-hour film about us, *The Aunties of Mingaletta*, with a grant from the Central Coast Council, which premiered during NAIDOC Week 2019. In the movie, introduced by Australia's first female Aboriginal federal MP Linda Burney, we described our struggles and our determination to educate the next generation and preserve our culture. It was so warmly received, I was absolutely thrilled.

Internationally, too, we were causing a stir. In 2020, the German government apologised officially to Aboriginal people in Australia for its consulate in Melbourne refusing, back in 1938, to forward on that letter from my great-grandfather William Cooper protesting about the treatment of the Jewish citizens to the political leadership in Berlin. '[That] would have been the right and morally correct thing for a consulate official to do,' said Felix Klein, the Commissioner for Jewish Life in Germany, on behalf of Chancellor Angela Merkel. It was a day of real jubilation.

So many good things have happened to wipe out some of the

hurt of the past. Mum would have been so proud if she could have seen what I'd become, what I'd made of myself. I'd struggled in the days after her death, without anyone to look out for me, and life had been very cruel in so many ways. But I'd survived and, despite the hardships, I'd never become bitter. Even though I'd been stolen from my birth mother, I'd known the love of the most wonderful of adoptive mothers, so I'd been luckier than most. And yes, I'd been the victim of a great deal of violence but it made me stronger and more resilient, with the confidence to know I could withstand whatever life threw at me.

Along the way, I'd received some of the most precious of gifts, too. I'd experienced far more than any one person could reasonably expect in a lifetime, and was now fortunate enough to be using that experience to do great work for my community, both Aboriginal and non-Aboriginal. I'd been able to reinvent myself to be brave and bold, and eventually find peace, surrounded by the love of my big, beautiful family.

Finally, I'd discovered a proud Aboriginal heritage and was thrilled to be accepted as a member of a wonderful group of Australia's First Peoples, a true daughter of the river country. Home, at last.

Author's Note

It's taken me a long time to write this book, and it felt quite traumatic reliving many of the events of my life and doing all the heart-searching necessary to share my story with others.

So when my friends at Echo Publishing suggested that a writer should work with me to help shape my story, I was delighted. We talked about whether I'd want an Aboriginal writer to help me, or someone not necessarily of Indigenous heritage, but who was an experienced biographer, used to working with a range of different subjects and knowledgeable about Koori issues.

Since I'd spent nearly half my life completely unaware that I was a member of the First Nations people, it felt right to me that I choose a writer equally at home in both non-Indigenous and Indigenous cultures.

With that in mind, I was introduced to Sue Williams and

instantly felt comfortable with her. She's written about a number of Aboriginal people before, in her series of outback books, and wrote the biography of outback showman Fred Brophy who discovered, much later in life, like me, his Indigenous heritage.

Sue has also worked with Indigenous community volunteers and has completed a course in Aboriginal culture with – amazingly – my old friend and cousin Jimmy Little's late sister Betty, a successful educator, author and singer-songwriter in her own right.

It felt right to be working together, and I'm thrilled with how my book has finally come to life. I hope it will touch a chord in everyone who reads it, and will now inspire other people to tell their stories and have their voices heard.

Acknowledgements

I would like to thank everyone who gave me support and encouragement during the years it took to write this book.

Thanks, first of all, to my mum Val Westman, who so carefully kept all the photos from my life, some of which we've used for the cover (I'm clutching the rag doll she made, Molly) and the picture section inside. Without her, they would have been lost forever. Thanks to my family, too: my kids, grandkids and great-grandkids who never stopped believing in me, and knew that I could do this thing.

A big thanks to Julie Asprey, who was the first to see some of my writings, and to Cindy O'Casey, Jodi Storey, Brian Cook and Lucy Desoto for their help.

Then, of course, to my publisher Tegan Morrison and my great friend Benny Agius of Echo Publishing, and to writer Sue Williams.

Thanks also to my copyeditor Rod Morrison and proofreader Angela Meyer.

I'd also like to give a huge shout-out to Peter Read and Coral Edwards of Link-Up who helped me trace my birth parents and my first family and discover my Aboriginal heritage. They're doing such great work! And to Donnie Williams who saw so clearly my Aboriginality and put me in touch with them.

Aunty Jessica Atkinson encouraged me continually, saying I needed to write our stories and get them out there as it would help our young people live their best lives too, while Uncle Boydie was also always there for me, as was Aunty Sally, William Cooper's sister, whom I met in an old people's home in Geelong. It can be hard for stolen generation members to go back to their traditional communities and be accepted, so it's important they're always welcomed back and their return celebrated. It's always going to be a traumatic journey, and from all sides.

Through telling my story, I hope to encourage other Aboriginal people to aim high. If I can do this, an uneducated 'gin' from the mission, then anyone can achieve anything they set their mind to. I'd love more Aboriginal people to write their stories about loss of identity and the devastating consequences that have resulted from losing their cultural heritage, and then about their strength that got them through it and, hopefully, their path afterwards to a better life.